THE ART OF EMILY CARR

A song of the rolling earth, and of words according,
Were you thinking that those were the words, those
   upright lines? those curves, angles, dots?
No, those are not the words, the substantial words are in the
   ground and sea,
They are in the air, they are in you.

from *A Song of the Rolling Earth* by Walt Whitman

When I want to realize growth and immortality more I go back
to Walt Whitman. *Everything* seemed to take such a hand in the
ever-lasting on-going with him — eternal overflowing and spilling
of things into the universe and nothing lost.

Emily Carr in a letter to Ruth Humphrey, April 1938

I Emily Carr in her studio
SUNSHINE AND TUMULT
Overleaf 1

THE ART OF EMILY CARR

Doris Shadbolt

CLARKE, IRWIN / DOUGLAS & McINTYRE   TORONTO AND VANCOUVER

A joint publication of

Clarke, Irwin & Company Ltd.
791 St. Clair Avenue West
Toronto, Ontario
ISBN 0-7720-1255-5

Douglas & McIntyre Ltd.
1875 Welch Street
North Vancouver, B.C.
ISBN 0-88894-244-3

CANADIAN CATALOGUING IN PUBLICATION DATA
Shadbolt, Doris,
    The art of Emily Carr

    Bibliography: p.
    1. Carr, Emily, 1871-1945. I. Carr, Emily,
1871-1945. II. Title.
ND249.C3S5   759.11   C79-091148-5

Design by Reinhard Derreth
Photography by Michael Neill
Separations by Tri Scan Graphics Ltd.
Typesetting by Vancouver Typesetting Company Ltd.
Printing by Sampson Matthews Ltd.
Binding by T.H. Best Printing Company Ltd.

CONTENTS

For Jack, who helped me see

PREFACE

The intention of this book is to provide an overview of the art of Emily Carr and a fuller appreciation of her dimension as an artist than now exists. It presents a broad visual base for tracing the development of her form in relation to her thought processes, and makes extensive use of her writing in attempting an understanding of her art and her artistic stance.

I first encountered Carr's work when, as a junior employee of the Art Gallery of Toronto, I took part in the preparation for her large exhibition at that institution in 1943. Making thumbnail sketches of her paintings at that time helped impress on me the strong and individual character of her vision. Years later, when I was working at the Vancouver Art Gallery, Director Richard Simmins encouraged me to take advantage of its major Carr collection, and I began work that was to lead to a catalogue raisonnée of her art. That project was doomed to be left uncompleted, considering the lack to time to devote to it and the prolific and disparate nature of her output. But the work begun then formed a basis for the Carr Centennial exhibition of 1971, and in turn for this present publication.

I have many people and institutions to thank for helping me in this undertaking. The owners of Carr paintings have responded enthusiastically to the idea of the book and been willing to have them included among the reproductions. Without the full co-operation of the Vancouver Art Gallery, the task would have been impossible, and I wish to thank Director Luke Rombout for expressing that co-operation from the beginning; and among an always friendly and willing staff there I would mention Registrar Scott Watson, who made the collection accessible to my frequent requests. On the staff of the National Gallery of Canada, I would like to thank Charles Hill, Assistant Curator of Post-Confederation Art, for his consistently generous sharing of information; and Linda Street, who permitted me a most helpful reading of the section of her Master's thesis dealing with Carr's spiritual evolution and its relation to her art. My thanks also to Anne Morrison, who undertook a thoughtful and valuable reading of my manuscript; to Gerry Mossop, Art Curator of the Provincial Archives; Peter McNair, Curator of Ethnology, and members of the photographic department of the Provincial Museum of British Columbia — all of whom were generous in their assistance. Material from the Emily Carr papers in the Public Archives of Canada, the Special Collections Division of the University of British Columbia Library, and the files of the National Gallery of Canada has been used with the permission of the writers who have been quoted or the inheritors of the involved estates. Lastly I would like to acknowledge Jill Wade's careful research of available bibliographic material.

Doris Shadbolt

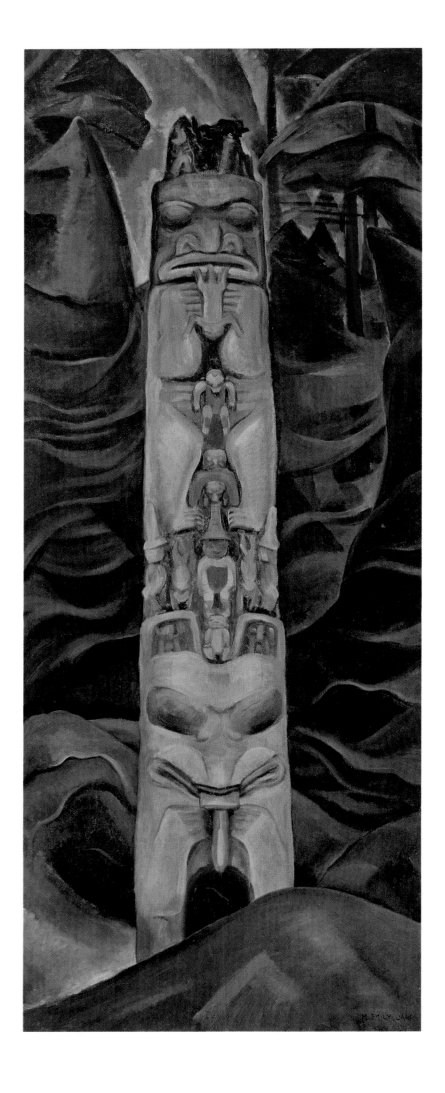

PROLOGUE

ARTIST OF THE CANADIAN WEST COAST   Emily Carr was born in Victoria on Vancouver Island 13 December 1871, died there 2 March 1945, and lived most of her life within a few blocks of the house where she was born in the James Bay district of that city. Her genius throve in the island's isolation from mainland British Columbia and in the province's isolation from the rest of Canada and the world. The two great themes of her work derived from the most characteristic features of that region — a unique and vanishing Indian culture, and a powerful coastal nature. It is logical to think of Carr and the Canadian West Coast at the same time, for her painting and her writing bear the indelible imprint of her long attachment to the place where she was born and where she chose to remain.

Despite persistent regional ties, she was not an artist who lacked broader contact, for as a girl in her late teens and early twenties she studied in San Francisco and spent altogether a little over three years there. Another five were spent in England and a little over one year in France at a time when some of the ideas crucial in the development of twentieth-century art were just emerging. Her work was admitted to a major Paris exhibition in 1911, where she was in the company of some of the progressive European artists of the day. There were trips to eastern Canada and to New York and Chicago. Through these travels she gained access to the general tradition of western European art within whose broad outlines she was to produce her work.

During one phase of her career, Carr painted in a French postimpressionist manner and at times revealed a distinctly Fauvist influence; during another period, her work showed stylistic links with Cubism. Late in her life, her passionate search for identification with universal primal energies produced occasional paintings that evoke van Gogh or suggest spiritual affinities with German Expressionism. Closer to home, her relationship to Canadian art and to the work of Lawren Harris and other members of the Group of Seven can be more readily observed. Yet she remained a highly individualistic artist, never truly part of larger world movements or their Canadian expressions, even though from time to time she borrowed their mannerisms.

Her long and productive career was marked by interruptions in style and continuity. She made a conventional early start and then, in her early middle age, a courageous and promising break into a larger international art stream, but at that point she lost her momentum in a sudden lapse of spirit. This lapse, though prolonged, was only a prelude to an explosive burst into sudden authority and a brilliant late flowering. Despite a substantial body of early work of interest and quality, that for which she is best known — and justly so — was done between her fifty-sixth and seventy-first years — paintings of dark and silent forests, monumental Indian carvings, towering trees, wild storm-tossed beaches and infinite skies, which spring from her lifelong Pacific coast experience.

THE WOMAN BEHIND CARR'S WRITING   Happily, Carr's urge for expression also took the form of writing. She produced five books of stories and reminiscences, as well as her published Journals, and fortunately some of her letters have now been deposited in public collections where they are available for study. The material is largely autobiographical, and in addition to its intrinsic interest and merit as writing, it reveals much of the person behind the artist.

The books were written some time after the events they recounted, however, and the uncertain process of memory, heightened — even distorted — by her literary skill and sense of drama, has made them unreliable sources for biographical detail. She frequently understates her age and is given to self-dramatization and idealization. The pieces in *Klee Wyck* are based on her experiences with Indians and on visits to Indian communities, but they are also stories in which time collapses and events are reshaped and interpreted to make a point in a story rather than to provide documentation.

Growing Pains is subtitled "The autobiography of Emily Carr," but it is really a collection of episodes recalled in later life when self-mythologizing had become habit, and there is no attempt to bridge the large gaps in time that separate the episodes. Even though information culled from her books of sketches and stories must be sifted and examined cautiously, it is invaluable for glimpsing her life and for seeing the face she wanted to show the world.

Hundreds and Thousands, the title she chose for her published Journals, refers to tiny English candies, so small they must be consumed by the mouthful to be appreciated. The Journals offer especially reliable information, and one wishes they had been begun before 1927 when she was already fifty-six. Still, they illumine the mature and important years of her painting life. They were intended for publication, and at times there is a self-consciousness about the writing as if she were aware of the reader looking over her shoulder, but on the whole the Journals are a spontaneous reflection of her mood and spirit and are, to a lesser degree, a record of her activities. Their form and style vary with her state of mind: rich descriptive passages followed by outbursts of frustration; thoughts on painting; soul searchings; reminiscences — broken by long silences. They represent an important personal and passionate manifesto, full of contradiction and at times irritating in their diffidence but nonetheless a powerful confession of artistic faith.

Carr was also a compulsive letter-writer and she knew that "there is a side of friendship that develops better and stronger by correspondence than contact, especially with some people who can get their thoughts clearer when they see them written. Another thing — that beastliness, self-consciousness, is left out, shyness, shamedness in exposing one's inner self there face to face before another, getting rattled and mislaying words. The absence of the flesh in writing perhaps brings souls nearer."[1]

As a correspondent who greatly needed to feel in close communication with absent friends, she had the knack of writing on a moment's impulse with a directness of speech and from the edge of her thought. The letters cover a wide range, depending on the recipient. With some correspondents she reported on day-to-day events and exchanged gossip about acquaintances; naturally she was particularly interested in the activities of fellow artists.

Unfortunately Carr's many letters to Lawren Harris, written between the late 1920s and early thirties, have not turned up to date; it is believed that he did not keep them. Harris, this leading Canadian artist, whom she met in Toronto in 1927, became the most important single influence in her artistic life. Her letters to him were obviously earnest communications about religion and work, and they revealed her insecurity in both these areas at that time.

This is made clear by his letters to her which were, as she was to comment when going through old correspondence many years later, "almost all work, one artist to another."[2] Many of Carr's letters are still in existence, however, and there are snappy letters to art gallery officials concerning their alleged mismanagement of matters relating to the shipping, exhibiting or purchasing of her paintings, which can be found in the files of several art institutions.

There are also letters containing emotional outpourings which reveal her misery and loneliness in her old age. This was particularly the case in the letters to her friend and mentor Ira Dilworth. They became friends, and it was he who brought her first book to the attention of Oxford University Press and edited all her later manuscripts. Carr met Dilworth when he was regional director of the western division of the Canadian Broadcasting Corporation. After her death he became her literary executor and, like Lawren Harris, one of the trustees of her estate. In her correspondence with him she touchingly splits herself into two personae: Small (which figures in the title of one of her books and was a name Dilworth used when writing to her), the imaginative, free child spirit in her; and Emily, the pragmatic, aging and sometimes, by her own admission, mean and nasty self. With this dual personality she could claim the privileges of a close relationship and yet, when necessary, be an ordinary, practical person, and give vent to frustration and anger.

The letters are written with whatever was handy and at any time: in pencil, on scraps of paper torn from notebooks, on board ship, in bed. And, demonstrating a characteristic lack of concern for providing peripheral information, the letters are often dated only "Sunday" or "midnight," or "3 a.m." Together they constitute a vivid and often moving portrait of a woman who, her provincialism and streak of sentimentality notwithstanding, possessed an individuality and strength of character that marked all she said and did.

Carr tells of her birth during a December snowstorm: "Contrary from the start, I kept the family in suspense all day. . . . I dallied. At three o'clock in the morning I sent Father" out in the snow for help.[3] She is evidently satisfied with this early display of will against her father, who ordinarily got his way in everything. Her account appeals as delightful story-telling and it also points to an essential attribute in her make-up: her unshakeable sense of self. Her confidence in her abilities was shaken at times but never her confidence in herself. The autobiographical component of her writing implies this sureness, a characteristic that is frequently brought out as she observes her difference from others. Her impatience, her rebelliousness, her contrariness run through *The Book of Small* and *Growing Pains* almost like a leitmotif. She was naughty as a child and lacked restraint as a young girl. As an adult she resisted the nice Victorian social conventions, scorned religious piety and dutiful good works, expressed her real feelings in angry outbursts. She smoked, rode astride a horse rather than sidesaddle, kept a monkey. She claimed that when she returned from a five-year stay in England as a woman in her early thirties, Victorians found her disappointingly unchanged. Instead of "an English Miss with nice ways," she wrote, "I was more *me* than ever, just pure me."[4] Clearly she felt her difference as strength, a needful attribute for defence against a society in which narrow-mindedness prevailed.

A reflection of the difference she felt was the large number of they's who loomed in her life: those who in one way or another formed the opposition. They included do-gooders, society ladies, clergymen with empty rhetoric, fussers, analysts, statistic-minded curators, critics and the affected. They were the snobs (though it might be said that she had her own inverted form of snobbery). They were the convention-bound (though from her upbringing she had retained her own set of conventions), who naturally belonged to the vague mass of those who were uninterested in or hostile to her work.

Whatever the dramatic licence in her writing and however much she enjoyed her eccentricity, she was different. In small and large ways she forced her will on the patterns of her life. Some of the small ways made her conspicuous in Victoria's everyday world, and those with a small-town attitude regarded her as someone outside the pale of ordinary society, something of the village oddity. The supreme statement of her difference was, of course, her stance as artist, and her Journals repeatedly confirm how completely she committed all her resources and personality into being that artist: her enormous will, her obstinacy, her sensory vitality, her sublimated erotic energy, her observation of nature and her identification with its forces, her yearning for spiritual fulfillment, her immense need for self-expression.

And, not unexpectedly, it was the greater difference entailed in being a dedicated artist that had more serious consequences for her. In periods of low self-confidence or dejection, the exhilaration of aloneness as a working condition turns into the pain of loneliness as a living condition. "I haven't one friend of my own age and generation. I wish I had. I don't know if it's my own fault. I haven't a *single thing* in common with them. . . . None of them like painting and they particularly dislike my kind of painting. . . . Oh Lord, I thank Thee for the dogs and the monkey and the rat."[5]

At a crucial time in her career her dialogue with Lawren Harris gave her immeasurable sustenance. His letters continued their patient, generous support and encouragement, though after a while he began writing advance disclaimers and reassurances into them against the hints of criticism she might find there, for he understood her great sensitivity and her insecurity within the artistic isolation she chose. The years of correspondence and the occasional visit with him were the only times while her art was still forming that she had a friend with whom she could communicate deeply and sympathetically about the things that mattered most to her. Later, when they had ceased to correspond regularly, a chance visit from a European artist drew the comment: "It is wonderfully heartening to speak with another artist. I have missed the contact with Lawren bitterly. To both of us religion and art are one."[6]

At the end of 1939 when she had just turned sixty-nine she felt that there was not one solitary soul she could open up to. There were others in her life besides Harris — towards the latter part, many others — who bolstered her spirits; but throughout the Journals and in many of her letters, especially those to Ira Dilworth, with whom she had a close bond in the last years, along with the moments of elation or contentment runs the theme of the artist's loneliness. Once when she had been reading *The Autobiography of Alice B. Toklas*, she wrote: "Oh, if there was only a really kindred spirit to *share* it with [the lagoon at sunset], that we might keep each other warm in spirit, keep step and tramp uphill together. . . . all the artists there in Paris, like all the artists in the East, jogging along, discussing, condemning, adoring, fighting, struggling, enthusing, *seeking* together, jostling each other, instead of solitude, no shelter, exposed to all the 'winds' like a lone old tree with no others round to strengthen it against the buffets. . . . It must be my fault somewhere, this repelling of mankind and at the same time rebelling at having no one to shake hands with but myself. . . . Stop this yowl."[7]

Still, her difference and aloneness were strengths to draw from, and one concludes that she acquired toughness in a climate of adversity, even if she had to help create it. She needed response to her work and longed for success, but when compliments came her way she often thought them cloying or insincere, or plain rubbish when they emanated from art critics who were inclined to be analytical or "aesthetical." Easiest to accept were compliments from ordinary people of no importance in the art world (and therefore incapable of conferring success on her), who were exercising no judgement on her work but simply responding intuitively. After a party in her studio at which her guests appeared to like her paintings, she confided: "All that 'goo' trickles over me and runs down the other side and makes not one indentation. I do not think it is empty flattery. I think most of them *felt* something but it kind of nauseates me. I liked the little Chinaboy's remarks much better, badly expressed but from his heart."[8]

Failure was painful, but she knew how to deal with it and so sometimes interpreted events negatively when they could have been read otherwise. She speaks of the response she had had to her solo exhibition in Seattle late in 1930, some of it warmly congratulatory; yet when she had not heard from the gallery's director six weeks later she concluded that the show was not a success and read herself a moral lesson: "It did me good to have to rattle around and work and get ready for it. The fact that it fell flat was good for my conceit. If the work had been big enough — hit the bull's-eye — people would *have* to acknowledge it." She goes on to berate the "lazy minds and shrinking hearts of us who shirk the digging grind,"[9] exhorting herself to continue the struggle.

Like most artists, she wanted success but feared what it might do to her and to her work, and so for much of her life she created a protective shell to guard against flattery, minimizing success when it came her way. Her concept of the creative process — and of life itself, as she was fond of reiterating — is that of a never-ending struggle; she feared that success might make her smug and would interfere with her self-criticism. Also, she found the equation that relates paintings and "filthy money" repellent; she knew that art and money belong to different aspects of life and cannot be meaningfully equated, and that if she began to see the "dollar sign"[10] as she worked, she would lose her bearings as an artist.

More frequently in later years, when her confidence was stronger and the risks involved were less, she was able to resolve the conflict and could gauge and accept her successes. In February 1936, as she was packing to leave the memory-filled House of All Sorts, and in a mood of reminiscence and self-analysis, she faced the ambivalence in herself. "When I look over things I see that I have been careless over my receipts. I have had lots of recognition. Way over West it has come to me and I have not properly appreciated it. Why? It did not seem to mean much to me. I was wasteful of it, did not follow it up. I might have, and perhaps would have, become well off and financially successful. Things were suggested but I let them slip, was saucy over them. Now bad times have come; I cannot reach the public and the public soon forget. Some tire and look for a new person of interest. I would not kowtow. I did not push. Praise embarrassed me so that I wanted to hide. You've got to meet success half-way. I wanted it to come all the way, so we never shook hands."[11]

THE PAINTING AS AUTOBIOGRAPHY Carr's writing, which achieved popularity before her painting, reveals the intense individuality of this woman who lived the life of an artist — as much as her upbringing and her abilities would allow — fully, romantically, passionately. And so, in addition to the rich legacy she left behind as painter and author, she emerges as a fascinating human being. Although it is not the perspective of this book to portray the woman Emily Carr, an understanding of her work is inseparable from some knowledge of her life. Not to recognize the auto-biographical nature of her evolving art, the sense in which her painting is the most powerful expression of her existence and a necessity of her life, is to miss one of the dimensions of her work.

Her art is autobiographical not in the superficial sense that it follows her movements and relates to periods of her life, nor as a reflection of her changing moods. It is in the nature of some art to find its sources in the deepest wellspring of the self, and so it was with Carr in her mature work, once she had learned to make that mysterious connection with her intense psychic energy. She was one of those artists who, in the words of the psychoanalyst Otto Rank, live themselves out completely in their work.

II Carr as a young girl

THE VICTORIA ENVIRONMENT The opportunity for becoming — and remaining — an artist had to be created by Carr herself, for neither her family nor the community in which she grew up provided the kind of nurturing environment that was based on recognition of art's vital role in a culture or that accepted the artist as a totally committed person.

The Canadian Far West is isolated from eastern centres by distance, and the barrier of the Rocky Mountains on one flank and the Pacific Ocean on the other make it a geographically separate territory as well; until 1871, when Emily Carr was born, it was also a politically distinct territory. In that year British Columbia, whose settlement lagged well behind that of Ontario and Quebec, became a Province of the Dominion of Canada, with Victoria as its capital. The gold rush to the interior of the province in the latter half of the 1850s and the 1860s had helped make Victoria a bustling frontier town; thriving businesses in shipping, trade and supplies for miners catered to a mixed population of British, Americans, American Negroes, Chinese, West Indians, native Indians and many other nationalities. By 1871, however, Victoria had fewer than 8,000 inhabitants and was already falling behind the mainland's Vancouver as the vital centre of the province.

In 1886 the first trans-Canada train arrived in Vancouver from the east — the last link in that expensive steel chain designed to make one country out of widely distant regions. The railway signalled the beginning of better communication with the rest of the nation, but goods, people and ideas still travelled slowly. A five- or six-hour ferry trip across the Strait of Georgia was required to reach Victoria, whose coveted English tone, customs, connections and allegiances only emphasized its geographical introversion. Though the seat of government was located there, it was a community without a university and lacked the general ferment of ideas and intellectual activity found in longer-settled and more cosmopolitan centres. The Victoria in which Carr grew up was far too young to reflect, in its attitudes or its institutions, any notion that art could be a serious vocation. There were, of course, itinerant artists, engineers and topographers who sketched the scenery, and inevitably a few painters, possibly skilled but amateur in their attitude to art. Usually their painting took the form of gentle watercolour renderings of nature in the British tradition; Carr herself was to produce in this style for a time. Such painting could be accepted as appropriate leisure-time activity, something to be taught in private classes or ladies' schools, but it was thought to have little to do with the real business of life.

Towards the end of the century an interest in art was shared by enough people in Victoria and Vancouver to encourage the formation of sketching groups and exhibiting societies. Fall fairs in Victoria included art displays along with the exhibits of livestock and agricultural, industrial and other products that made up these annual events. Carr's work was first shown in the 1894 Fall Fair on her return from school in San Francisco. The Island Arts Club, which held its first exhibition in 1910, became the Island Arts and Crafts Club, and finally the Island Arts and Crafts Society, an organization on which she was to vent much scorn. It members were limited in their notion of art (they were steeped in the British watercolour tradition) and many joined partly for social reasons. The lists of exhibitors in the early years of the IACS show the degree to which art was a woman's activity: an indication of the limited interest in art at that time. Mention should be made of Sophie Pemberton, a close contemporary of Carr. She had been trained at the Slade in London and painted seriously, but her work was not distinctive enough to challenge, or raise the level of local understanding. She was, however, to help Carr indirectly later on.

Though Carr eventually found more important outlets for her work farther afield, they were not frequent enough, and response to them was not sufficiently immediate, for her needs; she continued to exhibit with the IACS until 1941, in spite of her dislike

III Carr in the Cariboo
IV Family Picnic, 1889

for the organization and the chatty tea parties connected with their shows. The need to objectify the fruits of one's creativity by putting them out into the world is not the only indication of seriousness, but it is a fundamental one, and Carr responded to it, inviting public judgement from the beginning. Such exhibiting opportunities as Victoria had to offer helped answer this need at the simplest level (she supplemented them with her own studio exhibits), though they could not confer on her work more than local significance. Even in 1939 she was to complain to the Director of the National Gallery in Ottawa: "The Arts and Crafts Society are like a necklace of millstones around the neck of art. . . . I think Victoria is the most hopeless place in the Dominion."[1] At the time of Carr's death, Victoria still had no civic gallery, though the city had turned down a 1929 offer of a private collection along with funds for one. By then, of course, Carr had long since established connections with other parts of the country from which she drew moral and critical support.

Vancouver in the first decade of the century was perhaps a little more advanced. The Vancouver Studio Club, where Carr exhibited and where, between 1905 and 1910, she taught classes, became at the end of 1909 the first chartered art society in the province (the British Columbia Society of Fine Arts), and this formality gave its exhibitions a somewhat more professional standing. By 1925 the city had an art school which brought in as teachers such highly respected artists as F.H. Varley and J.W.G. Macdonald. By 1931 it had a public gallery. Even so it was far behind the older eastern Canadian cities of Toronto and Montreal where a climate for art had long existed and where innovative artists could show their work in various clubs, societies and galleries amid an atmosphere of lively discussion. Towards the end of the century's second decade, the Group of Seven was taking the Ontario art world by storm, but ten years later Carr had still not heard of them.

HOME AND FAMILY   Nothing in Emily Carr's family background suggested that from it a major artist would emerge. Her father, Richard Carr, whose strength of character and bold spirit were evidently passed on to his youngest daughter, had left England as a poor, uneducated young man in his late teens to seek adventure and fortune. His diary[2] tells of his thirteen years' wandering before settling in 1849 in Alviso, California. There he developed a prosperous business supplying gold miners. And there he met the English girl Emily Saunders whom he married on a subsequent trip to England in 1855. In July 1863 he and his family, which by then included Edith and Clara, arrived in Victoria, where he built a successful business on Wharf Street in wholesale groceries and liquors. In his fine large house — today the Emily Carr Arts Centre, a designated heritage site — on the present Government Street (which absorbed the original Carr Street) he and his wife provided a stable, comfortable and well-run household for their family. Seven other children were born in Victoria: three sons who died in infancy, then Elizabeth (Lizzie), Alice, Emily and Richard. Richard, of whom Emily was very fond, died of tuberculosis at the age of twenty-three.

When Emily was a child, the family property was semi-rural; the Carrs had pets, a large garden and a barn for their cow and horse. Only a fence separated the property along one of its boundaries from Beacon Hill Park, with its abundant growth, cliffs, driftwood beaches and seascape as well as its view of the American Olympic Mountains. Such an environment was bound to nourish the imagination of a sensitive girl, and Carr describes in *The Book of Small* and elsewhere her childhood pleasure in nature and her empathy with animals. In *Growing Pains* she acknowledges a debt to Johnny, the family's former circus pony, who provided her with a means of getting away from town to the "deep lovely places that were the very foundation on which my work as a painter was to be built."[3]

We learn too from Carr's writing that in the Victoria society to which her family belonged, religion played an important role and provided authority for moral behaviour. It also loomed uncomfortably large in her home life, where there were regular morning family prayers and Bible readings, frequent visits by one sister's missionary acquaintances, and Sunday School classes organized by another sister. Sunday was a special day comprised of a series of rituals which began on Saturday night after Bong, the Chinese boy servant, had washed up and gone home.

Clearly Carr's growing-up period was rich, and the family ties were strong and loving, yet she thought of herself as the disturbing element. "Outsiders saw our life all smoothed on top by a good deal of mid-Victorian kissing and a palaver of family devotion; the hypocrisy galled me. . . . The others were prim, orthodox, religious."[4]

Carr's family, she claimed, had never produced an artist nor even known one, but at least the notion of a young girl learning art as a social accomplishment and as part of her education was accepted by her parents. She was allowed to take drawing lessons as a child and again later with her sisters on Fridays after the regular classes at Victoria High School. She liked to draw heads, and her habit of drawing faces on her fingernails, pinafores and textbooks contributed to her reputation as a refractory pupil.[5] She also purchased some plaster casts of human features — noses, hands, lips and eyes — which she had seen being used as models by a Victoria tombstone maker, and these she drew over and over again. Her description of her early art activities reflects a real and natural inclination: "Father pruned the cherry tree under our bedroom window. The cherry sticks were twisty but I took three of the straightest, tied them at one end and straddled them at the other and put two big nails in the wood to hold a drawing board. With this easel under the dormer window of our bedroom I felt completely an artist."[6]

Her mother, who was in delicate health and on whose sympathetic nature Carr relied, died in 1886 when the strong but vulnerable girl was fourteen. Her father, who had been in his early fifties when she was born, was to die two years later. "An ultra Englishman till he died,"[7] he emerges in all Carr's writing as the strong and authoritarian centre of the family. The deep childhood bond she felt with him was broken when in her early teens he disgusted her with his "bestial brutalness of explanation"[8] about the facts of reproduction. The resulting hatred she carried against him softened in later years after she read his diary; and when *The Book of Small* was published, she expressed the hope that her respectful writing about him had "sort of squared her with him [and] atoned for all the years of bitterness." Still, she says, "I loved Mother best."[9]

When she asked her guardian, James Hill Lawson, for permission to attend an art school in San Francisco it was doubtless partly to escape the authoritarianism of Edith, the oldest sister who was now running the household. But Carr was also able to persuade Lawson that her interest in art was very real and had been growing for some time. She herself could not have known what it meant to be an artist or what struggles lay ahead, but she had made a start.

Notwithstanding antagonisms and misunderstandings, she was to retain close family bonds with Lizzie and Alice, the two sisters nearest to her in age and who, like her, lived out their lives in Victoria. But despite an increasing interdependence and fondness for each other as they grew older, there was an area of interest that the two sisters could not share with Emily — her art. For artistic understanding, exchange and moral support she had to turn elsewhere.

EARLY ACCOMPLISHMENTS

SAN FRANCISCO   "Long rows of students sat with lap-boards which had straddled hind legs that rested on the floor. Other students stood at easels drawing. In the centre of the room under a skylight were great plaster images on pedestals. . . . Art School was not exactly what I had expected but this was a beginning and I was eager to attack the big plaster foot they set before me to draw."[1]

"San Francisco did not have much to offer in the way of art study other than the school itself, no galleries, no picture exhibitions. Art was just beginning out west. The school was new. Students came here to make a start."[2]

In the late summer of 1890 Carr entered the California School of Design, which was then located over the public market on Pine Street — a dusty, dilapidated, crowded place, the casual atmosphere of which she enjoyed. There were social obligations, and three of her sisters spent about a year with her in the city, but she worked hard. The school's approach to art training followed the conventions of the time, and she progressed from the drawing of antique casts to still life. Such was the prudishness of her upbringing in Victoria, though, that she could not bring herself to take the next step and enter the life class with its nude models; that had to wait until some nine years later when she was studying in London. Of all the classes in San Francisco, she liked best the optional weekly outdoor sketching sessions in vacant lots, cow pastures or among stretches of fence and bush. "Sketching outdoors was a fluid process, half looking, half dreaming, awaiting invitation from the spirit of the subject to 'come, meet me half way.' . . . Atmosphere, space cannot be touched, bullied like the vegetables of still life or like the plaster casts."[3]

After three years and a few months she returned to Victoria, bringing with her work which was "humdrum and unemotional — objects honestly portrayed, nothing more."[4] Nothing had happened at the school to enlarge her awareness of art and life. This is borne out by comparing two drawings that were separated by five years including the time spent in San Francisco. The first is a charming pencil drawing, *Portrait of a Child,* done in 1890, probably from a photograph, which shows a considerable natural skill in drawing; the other is a precise ink rendering of *Rock Bay Bridge,* done in August 1895. In different media they show the same straightforward representational approach to their subjects, the one she also uses in the drawings and watercolours executed in Ucluelet in 1898.[5]   The latter had the added interest of representing her first involvement with an Indian theme.

On her return from San Francisco Carr organized children's art classes in her first studio, the patched-up loft of the cow barn. She was in her early twenties and still the baby in a household of sisters whose interests and pursuits differed from her own, and the strain of living at home had not diminished. But neither had her interest in art, and she decided to go abroad to further her studies. "I slung an old pair of shoes across the studio rafters. When pupils paid me I shoved the money away in my shoes. . . . When . . . [they] were crammed with money . . . I announced, 'I am going to London.' "[6]

ENGLAND   She chose London over Paris or Rome because it did not present a language problem, and it was also a natural choice for someone who had grown up in British-oriented Victoria. In the late summer of 1899 she set out by rail across Canada, armed with a "bale of introductory letters asking people to be kind."[7] She subsequently questioned her decision, for the Westminster School of Art, which she entered in the fall of 1899, was plodding and uninspired, and she thought the London art world conservative. Although she found a lot to interest her in the city, particularly the little corners that she poked into by herself, she says, "cities did not sit on me comfortably. . . . the oldness and history of it [London] made little appeal to me."[8]

M. EMILY CARR. 1909.

An obsessed worker, she followed the school's day-long life classes with evening classes in design, anatomy and clay modelling. More rewarding for her art, and obviously more enjoyable, were the times she spent outside London. There was a summer vacation in Berkshire, where she joined a class and had her first English outdoor sketching experience. Looking back, she believed that she had learned a lot there where the distances were softened by haze and the "colour did not throb so violently."[9] Then there was a term in the art colony at St. Ives, Cornwall, where she joined the group working primarily in sea and landscape painting under the Swede Julius Olsson. This was a stimulating situation, for Olsson's views were at variance with those of his assistant, Algernon Talmadge, with whom he took turns at criticism. The energetic Olsson wanted his students to paint the white boats and sea, and with full sunlight on the canvas. Talmadge respected Carr's empathy for the hidden, quiet places which led her to prefer the haunting, solemn, ivy-draped Tregenna Wood behind the village, and he recognized the quality of the studies she did there.

In the spring of 1902 she went to the Meadows Studios in Bushey, Hertfordshire, where the land "dipped and rose pastorally and was dotted with sheep, cows and spreads of bluebells. Everything was yellow-green and pearly with young spring. Larks hurried up to Heaven as if late for choir practice."[10] There again she painted in a little wood, and her teacher, John Whitley, left her with an important lesson: "The coming and going of foliage is more than just flat pattern. . . . there is sunshine too in the shadows."[11]

The last eighteen months of her five-year stay in England were spent miserably in a Suffolk sanatorium where she was seriously ill, a period she later put to literary use in her book *Pause*. That book is the only concrete accomplishment surviving from her stay in England, for the paintings have largely disappeared. Perhaps some were left behind in a country where they would have been undistinguished except to those who valued them for personal reasons. Others were destroyed later, long after her return to Canada, along with letters and mementos of the many friendly contacts she made there and remembrances from her student years in San Francisco and France as well. Her early habit of spontaneous drawing — quick sketches illustrating or caricaturing moments in life's little dramas — has provided some delightful recollections of this period: drawings done in the sanatorium or elsewhere on her travels. Often she herself is the subject of these sketches, viewing herself with amusement just as later she gently ridicules herself in her writing. Apparently her attempts to see herself honestly, clearly and often with ironic humour gave her strength in dealing with the world.

Carr arrived back in Victoria in mid-October 1904, having spent a month visiting friends on their ranch in the Cariboo cattle range country of central British Columbia. There she roamed the land, "mounted on a cow-pony,"[12] visiting an Indian settlement, enjoying the animals, wild and domesticated, and being restored by the air and space of the Canadian West.

VANCOUVER, VICTORIA   Depressing and unproductive though the English sojourn had been, it did not alter her view of herself as artist, and once back in British Columbia she set about organizing her life for her art. A city directory lists her as living in the old Carr house in 1905, and during eight months that year she did a series of political cartoons for the weekly newspaper *The Week*. By early 1906 she was in Vancouver, where she had gone in response to a request to teach at the "Ladies' Art Club of Vancouver," actually the Vancouver Studio Club and School of Art. She rented a studio at 570 Granville Street and remained in the city until midsummer of 1910, living a full and busy life, teaching and painting.

During these years she produced many watercolours: the gentle scenery in and around

Stanley Park at that time was just seven miles of virgin forest, three quarters surrounded by sea. Alone, I went there to sketch, loving its still solitudes — no living creature but dog Billie and me, submerged beneath a drown of undergrowth. Above us were gigantic spreads of pines and cedar boughs, no bothersome public, no rubbernoses. Occasional narrow trails wound through bracken and tough sallal tangle. Underfoot, rotting logs lay, upholstered deep in moss, bracken, forest wastage. Your feet never knew how deep they would sink.

Growing Pains, pp. 207-08

27

Vancouver and Victoria, gardens, figure studies, flower pieces, all standard artistic fare, and she painted them sensitively and with intimacy of feeling. Still, they are evidence that her study in England had not awakened her latent powers. Her painting of this period was in fact not too different from that which she described rather scornfully in her autobiography many years later: "Browsing cows, . . . placid streams with an artistic wriggle meandering through pastoral landscape — that was the Old World idea of a picture."[13] She had not tried, nor had even thought of trying, to reproduce the vast, wild landscapes of the West, which she had been told were unpaintable. Her paintings at this time were mainly small in scale. It is fortunate that some were given to relatives or family friends, for she destroyed many others when her ideas of art had drastically changed.

However, interspersed with these gentle domestic scenes are paintings whose themes are very different: dim, solemn, woodland interiors, many of them painted in the magnificent forests of Vancouver's Stanley Park. And there are the first sketches of northern Indian settlements where native life was less debased than in the province's more populated southern reserves.

COMMITMENT TO THE INDIAN THEME   The early culture of the Canadian Northwest Coast Indians had been one of the world's most distinctive. But in Carr's time, the Indians, in their villages, settlements and reserves, showed in varying degrees their demoralization since the white man had taken over their lands. There were reserves on Vancouver Island, so that Indians were part of Victoria's life, idling on the streets, selling baskets, and, like "Wash Mary" who did the Carr family washing, doing menial jobs. But there still existed tangible testimony of the high period in Indian culture — houses, poles and masks — the art of a vigorous and inventive people living in a rich environment.

The Indian theme came into Carr's art through her interest in the people. She was probably attracted to them first because they lived outside the class of society whose narrow values she had already rejected. She was proud that she could get along with Indians, and she tells how, on an early visit to the village of Ucluelet on Vancouver Island, she and the chief came to know each other without benefit of words. "The stare of his eyes searched me right through. Suddenly they were done. . ."[14] He saw that she was not afraid of him, was not stuck up and was ready to laugh. Having to substitute pantomime for speech she had laughed, and the Indian gave her the name Klee Wyck, which means laughing one.

Her first Indian work — direct drawings and watercolours — was done on the Ucluelet trip that she made in 1898 in the company of a missionary friend of her sister. The portrait sketches and figure studies of the people, the scenes of the village and its life, reflected the devitalized state of native culture — a theme rich in human significance, if that was what she wanted for her art. Her interest in the Indian people continued, as portrait and figure sketches done on later trips indicate, but after 1912 figures disappeared from her painting as her artistic goals became clarified. Once she began to focus on the Indians' monumental sculptural art of earlier, more vital times, her art developed a new purpose. Carr dates her commitment to the Indian theme from 1907, when she and her sister Alice made a pleasure trip to Alaska. Seeing her sketching the Indian village at Sitka, an American artist said that there was true Indian flavour in her drawings, and this started her thinking. On the way back down the coast they passed many Indian villages. "The Indian people and their Art touched me deeply. . . . By the time I reached home my mind was made up. I was going to picture totem poles in their own village settings, as complete a collection of them as I could. . . . With this objective I again went up north next summer and each successive summer

during the time I taught in Vancouver. The best material lay off the beaten track. To reach the villages was difficult and accommodation a serious problem. I slept in tents, in roadmakers' toolsheds, in missions, and in Indian houses. I travelled in anything that floated in water or crawled over land."[15]

She made trips north in 1908, 1909 and 1910 to coastal settlements including Alert Bay, Tsatsisnukwomi and Cape Mudge, and to Lytton in the interior of the province. There is a small canvas dated 1909, and perhaps there are others; but for the most part the fruits of these trips were watercolours and drawings which, together with those from subsequent trips in 1912, 1928, 1929 and 1930, provided the basis for the large body of paintings on Indian subjects she produced during her painting life.

In her autobiography, *Growing Pains*, Carr says: "Indian art broadened my seeing, loosened the formal tightness I had learned in England's schools. . . . The Indian caught first at the inner intensity of his subject, worked outward to the surfaces. His spiritual spiritual conception he buried deep in the wood he was about to carve."[16] Her understanding of Indian art is not in fact reflected in her work until after 1927, when she strips the poles of excessive detail, removes them from distracting settings and concentrates on their sculptural strength and expressive energy. Until then she applies a style to the Indian subjects, either a straightforward, carefully observed and rendered watercolour style (as in the work of 1908-10) or the French-derived manner she was to bring back with her from Europe in 1911.

Her dedication to the Indian theme in these early years was important mainly because it provided her with a valuable moral and social purpose for her art, which in turn gave impetus and focus to her creative drive. The Indian theme was also sufficiently complex and compelling to engage her for many years, revealing deeper layers of meaning as her understanding of it developed.

CEDAR CANNIBAL HOUSE,
UCLUELET, B.C.
watercolour 8

SKAGWAY
watercolour 9

Untitled
oil on canvas   27a

PAINTING IN FRANCE   On 11 July 1910, Emily and Alice left Victoria for France, stopping in Calgary, Edmonton, Quebec and London. Carr had saved up for this trip while her classes were going well in Vancouver, and she was to stay in France from late summer until the fall of the following year. This period marks her entry into the central stream of twentieth-century art.

"I did not care a hoot about Paris history. I wanted *now* to find out what this "New Art" was about. I heard it ridiculed, praised, liked, hated. Something in it stirred me, but I could not at first make head or tail of what it was all about. I saw at once that it made recent conservative painting look flavourless, little, unconvincing."[1] What she found there — that is, what she could respond to and put to her own use — was Post-impressionism. She was not affected by the more innovative experiments then being undertaken by Braque, Picasso and others, nor is there anything to indicate that she was even aware of the revolutionary changes taking place at that vital moment in the evolution of modern art: changes that would shake art to its very foundations. There is nothing strange about this. The work of the more intellectual and theoretically advanced artists would have had little relevance for her simpler, more holistic needs, if she had encountered it. Besides, of the relatively short period of her stay in France, only a few months were spent in Paris itself. As usual, she preferred less populous and less sophisticated terrain.

Her chief artistic contact was Henry William Phelan Gibb, a "very modern"[2] English artist living and working in Paris, to whom she had been given a letter of introduction. Some of his pictures pleased, others shocked her. "There was rich, delicious juiciness in his colour, interplay between warm and cool tones. He intensified vividness by the use of complementary colour. . . . Mr. Gibb's landscapes and still life delighted me — brilliant, luscious, clean. Against the distortion of his nudes I felt revolt."[3] On his advice she took classes at the Académie Colarossi, where an instructor told her she was doing well and had good colour sense, and subsequently to a studio[4] where she could get criticism in her own language. However, she stayed only a short time in each place.

Following an illness and a recuperative trip to Sweden (did this wooded northern country remind her of home?) she joined a spring class in landscape painting given by Gibb in the little canal town of Crécy-en-Brie, not far from Paris. She clearly had a rapport with this teacher-mentor, who recognized her seriousness and her determination, and when he and his wife went to Brittany, she accompanied them, sketching for several months while staying in the little town of St. Efflam. In the fall, before returning to Canada, she worked for six weeks with a "fine" watercolourist teaching at Concarneau, probably the New Zealander Frances Hodgkins.[5] The relaxed pleasure Carr found in her experience of rural and small-town France is recorded in *Growing Pains* and reflected in the many small canvases and watercolours she did at the time.

Before her return to Canada she had two paintings accepted for hanging in the *Salon d'Automne* of 1911, Paris' large open-juried annual exhibition. Carr mistakenly referred to this as the rebel show, probably confusing it with the *Salon des Indépendents*, whose 1911 show, incidentally, included a concentrated showing of the Cubists, which virtually served as an announcement of their emergence as a group. Nonetheless her two paintings hung among select company, for included in the list of exhibitors were Archipenko, Bonnard, Bourdelle, van Dongen, Duchamp, Duchamp-Villon, Segonzac, La Fresnaye, Gleizes, Léger, André Lhote, Marquet, Maillol, Matisse, Pascin, Picabia, Redon, Rouault, Valadon, Vuillard — along with about six hundred others whose names have not so well survived the test of time. A fellow Canadian, James Wilson Morrice, was also there, and the program of exhibits included a retrospective showing of Pissarro.

35

At the time that Carr visited France, Postimpressionism was a diffused style, representing absorbed innovations of the Impressionists, the Postimpressionists, and, to the degree that it involved brilliant and arbitrary colour and violent brushwork, something of the Fauves. It was both a way of seeing and a manner of painting, and in common-enough practice by that time to be readily picked up and adapted to individual use. For Carr it was truly a way of "fresh seeing"[6] and although her French paintings are modest, they represent a major change in her work. For the first time she understood the distinction between what the eye sees out there "in nature" and the different kind of meaning shapes take on when translated to a flat picture plane. She began to use a palette of light and broken colour, employing contrasts in hue rather than tone; she also began a direct and often vigorous use of the brush, displaying a feeling for the substance of pigment and for flat pattern. Because it treated subjects as coloured sensation rather than as carriers of meaning or feeling, Postimpressionism offered Carr an appropriate way to handle her French subjects — village scenes, cottages, landscapes — since she herself was not yet ready to paint out of her deeper experience. She quickly developed a kind of colour shorthand for translating visual information, which gave her painting an energy and vibrancy appropriate to her mood at the time.

Apart from a few earlier works, prior to her departure Carr had painted in watercolour. Now she switched to oil, a medium that, because of its quality of substance, was in keeping with her new perception. Working directly she painted small canvases of the countryside and village scenes — farm yards, the canal at Crécy-en-Brie, the old church at St. Efflam, cottage interiors — simplifying and flattening, eliminating detail, creating form out of brush strokes of colour. At times the manner is evocative of Cézanne, of whom Gibb was an exponent, as in *Old Church at St. Efflam*; at others, as in the Canadian National Gallery's painting *Autumn in France*, the brushwork and colour are directed more to vibrancy and pattern.

However, she also painted in watercolour, and a corresponding change takes place in that medium. There are a number of sparkling Brittany scenes, some of interiors with women going about every-day tasks, which differ markedly from the watercolours of a couple of years earlier. Figures are comprehended as compositional units to be marshalled according to pictorial needs: brought dramatically forward into the picture plane; moved right, left, up or down; or cut off by the margin. Highlights and shadows become part of an overall tonal structure, not simply the means of representing the subject with convincing volume and depth.

The body of small paintings produced in France represented a considerable achievement, especially since she was ill or out of the country part of the time and moving about much of the rest. She painted with a vigour and assurance, and with a sensuousness and formal awareness new to her, that from then on became part of her artist's equipment.

THE FRENCH MANNER CONTINUED IN BRITISH COLUMBIA   Carr arrived back in Victoria on 11 November 1911 but saw immediately that it was impossible for her to work there. Early in 1912 she moved to Vancouver, opened a studio at 1465 West Broadway, where in March and April she gave a showing of her French paintings,[7] and prepared to pursue her career as artist while supporting herself by teaching. That year and the first few months of 1913 were a productive period. She did a large number of paintings using the bolder, more direct style she had learned in Europe, working from drawings and sketches of Indian subjects done previously, as well as from an abundant new crop gathered on an extensive summer trip in 1912 to the Queen Charlotte Islands and the Skeena River. This, by far her most ambitious sketching excursion so far, had been particularly fruitful. Some of the 1912 watercolours resulting

There was a farm down in the valley — house, stables and hayricks
formed a square. . . . A Breton matron in her black dress and white
cap came out of the house. . . . She was proud of her cosy home.
It was well-to-do, even sumptuous for a peasant. Fine brasses were
on the mantelshelf, a side of bacon, strings of onions, hanks of flax
for spinning hung from the rafters. There was a heavy, black table,
solid and rich with age, a bench on either side of the table, a hanging
lamp above. There was a great open hearth and, spread on flat stones,
cakes were baking before the open fire. . . .

Growing Pains, p. 223

from that trip declare themselves by their finished and consciously composed character to be studio paintings, developed from field material of a more hurried nature. There are many drawings and sketches in the Newcombe Collection of the Provincial Archives in Victoria which support this view — fragments, details and quick notes from which more developed watercolours could be done.

OLD CHURCH NEAR ST. EFFLAM
oil on card 13

CONCARNEAU
watercolour 14

Cumshewa (no. 47) is one example of such carefully worked-out watercolours. Its compositional facility, elegant foreground arabesques and touches of intense colour in a moisture-drenched atmosphere, demonstrate her new sophistication. Another indication of their studio origin is the group of figures in one of these paintings. With few exceptions the Haida villages, such as Cumshewa, were not inhabited by the time Carr visited them. It would not be impossible, of course, for her to have used as models Indians who accompanied her on visits, but it was her practice, as indicated in a number of sketches and paintings that can be paired, to add a figure group to the finished version.

Many of the oil paintings done at this time are small in size, and deal with a single pole or a section of one, achieving simplicity of form by limiting the complexity of the subject itself. In several of the medium-sized works, the flat Indian house-fronts which she used as subjects helped her to formalize and shift emphasis to the surface plane.

There are several large canvases, however, which indicate a heightened ambition and confidence. Two of these are *Tanoo*, over five feet in length, almost acid in its high-keyed colouring, and the more sober *Indian House Interior with Totems*. From time to time a flavour of one of the Postimpressionists whom she could have seen in Paris is suggested. There is a hint of Gauguin in *Potlatch Figure* (a small painting from which she was later to develop the large canvas *Potlatch Welcome*) in its colour, its patterning and its use of primitive imagery. *Alert Bay* (a painting that combines information from 1908 and 1909 sketches) is reminiscent of Cézanne in its use of warm/cool nacreous colour and its expression of architectonic serenity. In general, in these Indian paintings her flaked brush stroke and the assertion of pigment create a painterly immediacy, as they had in her French paintings. At times the colour is chalky and greyed, at others, clear and brilliant — again as in her French paintings. These are not on-location works but studio pieces worked out from existing material. In their decorative rhythms, in the spreading of colour to the edges of flattened forms, and in the emphasizing of negative spaces, they show her heightened awareness of design.

In the spring of 1913 Carr rented Drummond Hall in Vancouver and mounted a large exhibition of almost two hundred of her paintings on Indian subjects. She delivered a lengthy lecture in connection with the display in which she discussed the paintings, the villages depicted and the circumstances of her visits to them, as well as various aspects of Indian culture. She named a Dr. Peet as her source of information — presumably Stephen Denison Peet, 1830-1914, who wrote about American Indian religion and mythology. The lecture ends as it began, with a statement of high purpose: "I glory in our wonderful west and I hope to leave behind me some of the relics of its first primitive greatness. These things should be to us Canadians what the ancient Briton's relics are to the English. Only a few more years and they will be gone forever into silent nothingness and I would gather my collection together before they are forever past."[8]

Carr's French style was in fact at odds with her avowed task of recording totem poles in their native settings. That intent, her paintings reveal, had been transformed into a primarily artistic one. This point was correctly (if, for her, disappointingly) grasped when her request to H.E. Young, Minister of Education for the British Columbia government, to further finance her excursions into the northern Indian villages, and to purchase her collection, was turned down on the advice of a consulting anthropologist,

who found her work too vivid and brilliant to truly depict the coast villages. As it was, her respect for the Indian subjects as subjects and her concern to represent the Indian forms faithfully acted as a curb to her recently developed appetite for more arbitrary colour and less detailed form. And to see how far her French experience had taken her in grasping the spirit of direct colour painting from nature, we go to several Vancouver scenes painted in 1912 or early 1913 in which there was not the same need for faithful representation. *Sawmills, Vancouver* and *Vancouver Street* are brilliant small works which would be comfortable in the company of Fauve paintings of their generation.

FIFTEEN YEARS DORMANT   The French paintings that Carr showed in her Broadway Street studio in Vancouver in 1912 were very advanced for the British Columbia art scene, or indeed for any part of Canada. She had never really lacked attention from the local press, and as early as 1894 her entry in the Victoria Fair was praised by Victoria's *Daily Colonist*. Now a favourable review of the new, more challenging paintings appeared in the 25 March edition of *The Vancouver Daily Province*, which stated that "her technique is of great breadth and vigour." However there was also a hostilely critical letter from a correspondent to the same paper which drew a defensive reply from Carr. In her letter she said that some people had bought pictures from her studio showings and arranged to take lessons. She also pointed out that a "fleeting visit . . . and a casual glance at exhibitions is not enough to form an opinion . . . one must give it [modern art] serious study. Contrary to my having 'given up my inspiration' I have only just found it."[9]

The big exhibition of Indian paintings a year later also drew praise, but when reaction to her work was mixed, she found that the criticism negated the compliments. Criticism did not have to be written or spoken, for she would construe as disapproval the uncommitted silence of any viewers.

"Rejected" is the title she gave her chapter in *Growing Pains* to describe the reception accorded her art when she returned from France. Certainly from the point of view of public acceptance she had taken a great risk in changing her art so radically from the style for which she was known, and her natural sensitivity to criticism must have been heightened at this crucial time when she was launching into a new phase in her work. Perhaps the strong term "rejection" was simply her way of stating that there was not enough support to keep her going in Vancouver, an instance of her wanting "success to come all the way." She wrote: "Nobody bought my pictures; I had no pupils; therefore I could not afford to keep on the studio. I decided to give it up and to go back to Victoria."[10] This she did in the spring of 1913.

There followed a very difficult time in Carr's life: "a period somewhere around fifteen years dormant — all the art smashed out of me flat."[11] Her father's property had been sold, with a share going to each of the sisters. On her lot at 646 Simcoe Street, not far from the old family home, Carr built a small apartment house, keeping one suite, including a studio, for herself. Her intention to paint while supporting herself from the rental of the other three suites (at first only two) did not work out. The First World War came, rentals went down, living costs rose, and "no matter how I pinched, the rentals would not stretch over mortgage, taxes and living."[12] But it was her art that was dormant, not her other activities; since she could not afford help, she had to take on the roles of rental agent, janitor and manager. "I tried in every way to augment my income. Small fruit, hens, rabbits, dogs — pottery."[13] But later, she was able to turn the tribulations of running an apartment house to literary advantage in her book *The House of All Sorts* which vividly recalls the experience of those years.

The pottery Carr made consisted of simple, hand-formed unglazed pieces, mostly small, which she decorated with Indian designs. They sold well and she kept on making

15

16

17

41

them until 1930. She was careful to keep the designs authentic, which eased her conscience somewhat, for she regarded that aspect of the venture as an exploitation of Indian art.

Although for the first fifteen years of its existence the studio was not fully used, Carr continued to paint a little, and she maintained her public image as an artist by exhibiting in annual shows organized by local or regional art societies. She exhibited both oils and watercolours with Victoria's Island Arts and Crafts Society in 1913, 1916, 1924, 1925 and 1926. She exhibited in Seattle with the Seattle Fine Arts Society in 1924 (one of her submissions won an award) and again in 1925. In 1926 she had a solo exhibition in conjunction with Victoria's annual fair. Some of her entries in those exhibitions were produced prior to 1913 — Indian subjects or work done in France — but paintings entitled *Uplands, In the Park, Autumn Woods, The Big Pine, The Point, Arbutus Tree, Esquimalt* indicate that she was able to escape sometimes from the demands of running an apartment house to paint from nature.

These paintings are relatively small in scale and continue the painterly manner learned in France, that of simplifying a scene into a pattern of direct, forceful brush strokes of light, often high-keyed colour. One of these, an untitled canvas showing a clump of trees on a slope, seems to foreshadow some of her paintings of the thirties, with their whirling, active skies. Sometimes the paint is thin on the prepared card or canvas, emphasizing the graphic quality of the stroke; in others it is thick and spreading. Staying within the postimpressionist idiom, several variant approaches to form can be noted: a Cézannesque building of structure out of simplified planes; a highly decorative patterning of curved and flattened masses; and a use of the brush stroke to carry its own gestural movement. These formal characteristics can be found in the 1912-13 work, but now, applied to subjects within easy reach of her house — rocks, trees, cliffs — and freed from the more exacting representational demands of the Indian subjects, they are more clearly stated. Still, nothing appears to suggest a new thrust or direction. It is interesting to note Carr's use at this time of the recurrent theme of the single tree in rocky terrain seen in strong profile against sky or sea, a theme that was coincidentally familiar in the repertoire of the Group of Seven in their paintings of northern Ontario.

And so Carr's statement, made in retrospect, "I never painted now — had neither time nor wanting. For about fifteen years I did not paint,"[14] was not literally true. But it was true in spirit. Compared to her earlier work and her later compulsively prolific output, she produced little during this fifteen-year span and added to it no fresh creative energy. Art had ceased to be the primary drive of her life.

TZARTSISEUCOMY
(Tsatsisnukwomi)
watercolour   19

TSATSINUCHOMI B.C.
(Tsatsisnukwomi)
watercolour   20

HOUSE POST,
TSATSISNUKWOMI, B.C.
watercolour   21

TANOO, QUEEN CHARLOTTE
ISLANDS
oil on canvas   22

Beyond the little point there were three fine house fronts. A tall totem pole stood up against each house, in the centre of its front. When Jimmie cut away the growth around the foot of them, the paint on the poles was quite bright. The lowest figure of the centre pole was a great eagle; the other two were beavers with immense teeth — they held sticks in their hands. All three base figures had a hole through the pole so that people could enter and leave the house through the totem.

Klee Wyck, pp. 13-14

MEMALILAQUA, KNIGHT'S
INLET
oil on canvas 23

GUISDOMS
watercolour 25

CEDAR HOUSE STAIRCASE
AND SUNBURST
watercolour 24

INDIAN HOUSE INTERIOR
WITH TOTEMS
oil on canvas 26

23

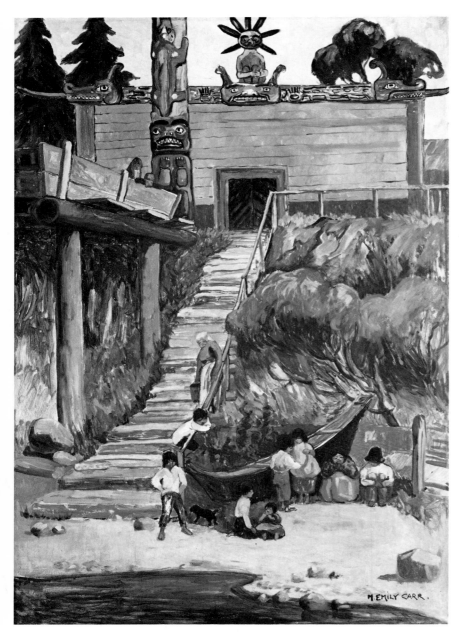

24

25

26

ARBUTUS TREE
oil on canvas 27

SAWMILLS, VANCOUVER
oil on gessoed canvas 28

ALONG THE CLIFF,
BEACON HILL
oil on card 29

28

27

29

VANCOUVER STREET
oil on card 30

CARR AT THE TURNING POINT

THE ARTIST AT AGE FIFTY-SIX   By the age of fifty-six Carr had demonstrated both in her art and in her attitude to it an independence and vigour shown by few Canadian artists she had known. She had produced a substantial body of work that was most notable for its large number of Indian paintings, whether carried out in her French or pre-French manner. Although she was not the only Canadian artist to have painted Indian subjects (at various times Statira Frame, Edwin Holgate, H. Bell-Smith and A.Y. Jackson did the same) for her the interest was sustained and not casual. Because her paintings were concerned with indigenous art, they were potentially attractive to an art audience with a taste for the exotic, as well as to one interested in ethnology and anthropology.

The paintings she did during the thirteen or fourteen years following the building of The House of All Sorts were not enough to substantially increase that body of work, nor do they represent any real development in her art. Had her painting career petered out, as it appeared to be doing by 1927, she would have won a place in the annals of regional art history but little more. However, given her potential and her as-yet-unfulfilled need for expression, it was inevitable that sooner or later she would free herself from the bondage of The House of All Sorts and return to full artistic activity.

Although she did not have a very wide following at this time, there were individuals interested in her and her work who were in a position to help her greatly. Dr. Charles Frederick Newcombe, a surgeon who was well-grounded in science and history, and passionately interested in the aboriginal inhabitants of British Columbia, had for some time been helpful, advising her and buying paintings. Ironically, it was his negative opinion as to the anthropological usefulness of her paintings that had resulted in the rejection of her proposal to the government in 1913, but his long-range support was very important to her. His son William Arnold (the reliable "Willie" of her book *Hundreds and Thousands*) inherited his father's interest in both Emily Carr and the Northwest Coast Indians, and he too was to become a constant supporter and collector of her work, as well as a close friend, and eventually a trustee of her estate. Today the Newcombe Collection, made up of works he and his father acquired from her — mostly drawings and watercolours of Indian subjects — resides in the Provincial Archives in Victoria where it forms one of the major public collections of her art.

Another early supporter was Harold Mortimer Lamb, an English-born mining executive and art enthusiast who settled on the Canadian West Coast. He wrote articles and letters championing the work of the Group of Seven, at that time the advanced art of English Canada, and protesting the neglect of western artists by the institutions of the east. Carr's work had been drawn to his attention by a professional Vancouver painter, Sophie Pemberton, and in 1921 he wrote to Eric Brown, Director of the National Gallery in Ottawa, commending her work.[1] Brown wrote back saying that he felt her work would be of more interest to the National Museum in Ottawa than to the National Gallery, and nothing further happened. Brown also heard about Carr from Dr. Marius Barbeau, famous ethnologist at the Museum and an authority on Canadian Northwest Indian culture. Carr's earlier sketching trips covered some of the same areas in which Barbeau had carried out research, and there he had heard of her activities. He had visited her several times in her studio and had probably spoken to Brown about her even before he had written to the Director in the fall of 1927. He purchased paintings on several occasions, and proved to be the kind of highly placed friend which she needed at a crucial time. Later he was to reproduce a number of her paintings — incorrectly identified as watercolours — in his two-volume work, *Totem Poles*.

1927 AND THE CRUCIAL TRIP TO EASTERN CANADA   In 1927 Eric Brown at last visited Emily Carr in her Victoria studio on Simcoe Street. So artistically isolated was she at this time that she "did not even know that Canada *had* a National Gallery"[2] and had never heard of the Group of Seven. This visit began the revitalization of her life and art in two ways. Brown invited her to participate in a forthcoming exhibition of West Coast Indian art at the National Gallery in Ottawa, and he told her of Frederick B. Housser's important book *A Canadian Art Movement*, which had already recorded the contribution to Canadian art history of the Group of Seven.

The purpose of the exhibition, Canadian West Coast Art, Native and Modern — the planning of which was already well under way at the time of her invitation — was "to mingle for the first time the art work of the Canadian West Coast tribes with that of our more sophisticated artists."[3] Carr, with twenty-six oils as well as pottery and rugs with Indian designs, was the best represented in the "modern" section, which also included paintings by the American Langdon Kihn, Walter J. Phillips, Edwin Holgate and A.Y. Jackson. The exhibition opened on 30 November under the joint sponsorship of the National Gallery and the National Museum of Canada and was subsequently shown in Toronto and Montreal. Some watercolours which Carr sent in the same shipment were not included in that show but were hung in the National Gallery's Annual Canadian Exhibition of 1928, and the Gallery purchased three of them.

This was the second time Carr had shown in an exhibition of more than regional significance, even though, as she herself realized, the context was ethnic rather than artistic. The first showing had been in the *Salon d'Automne* exhibition in Paris some sixteen years previously.

More significant even than the Ottawa exhibition was the trip Carr made to eastern Canada in connection with its opening. A Canadian National Railway pass had been given her, and she timed her journey so that she would have several days in Toronto prior to the opening, to meet the Group of Seven members and to see their work. Housser's book, which she had promptly bought at Brown's suggestion, had excited her enormously. Even so she could not have anticipated how thrilling the encounter would be and how important to her future. On the way she met F.H. Varley, who had been brought west to teach at the new Vancouver School of Decorative and Applied Arts; and later on she was to meet Franklin Carmichael and A.J. Casson. But Arthur Lismer, A.Y. Jackson, J.E.H. MacDonald and Lawren Harris received her in their studios in Toronto. Once the exhibition had opened, Harris reported to her that Jackson and Lismer felt that "though . . . [her] knowledge was poor, . . .[she] had got the spirit of the country and the people more than the others."[4]

Several days of meetings, viewing and socializing with other artists had been arranged for her, and on a second visit to Harris's studio, in response to one of her self-belittling remarks, he had said, "You are one of us."[5] One can imagine the stunning import for Carr of that simple statement. For the first time she could feel herself part of a community of dedicated, recognized artists, whom she knew to be great and who accepted the fact that her seriousness matched their own. Back on the coast and during the long years ahead, that sense of belonging to the serious art community would be stretched very thin at times, but never again would she suffer from the paralyzing feeling of isolation, or the loss of spirit that had retarded her art for nearly fifteen years. Speaking of her mood on returning from Toronto, she recalled in *Growing Pains*: "Sketch-sack on shoulder, dog at heel, I went into the woods singing. . . . household tasks shrivelled as the importance of my painting swelled."[6] In March 1928 she wrote Eric Brown that she was using gallons of paint and lots of canvas and was thrilled to be working at the Indian stuff again.

The burdensome House of All Sorts served Carr as home for an additional and artistically very productive nine years before she sold it and moved, on 2 March 1936, to a small rented cottage at 316 Beckley Street in a poor section of the same James Bay district of Victoria. Lizzie died in November of that year.

THE MATURE YEARS COMMENCE

"RELIGION AND ART ARE ONE"   The friendliness of the eastern artists and their warm encouragement of her art were reassuring to Carr, but the impact of their painting was overwhelming and left an indelible impression. Beside the work in their studios, she had seen the exhibition of the Royal Canadian Academy in Montreal which devoted one room to the paintings of the Group of Seven, and there she had studied them at leisure. Her response to individual members varied, but in general she was impressed by their largeness of vision and the boldness with which they handled their themes. She accepted so readily and naturally their identification of a Canadian spirit with areas of rugged, untamed Canadian landscape that she later took it for granted that an interest in the big Canadian spaces had been hers all along. In reality that interest is apparent in her painting only after her meeting with the eastern artists.

It was true, as Carr felt, that her paintings in the Ottawa exhibition — all of them dating from 1912 or 1913 — were small in concept and lacking in vision when compared with those of the Group of Seven. Their paintings sacrificed detail to bold statement, and their strong design served an expressive purpose which she found forceful and convincing. Hers was an art, at that point, of painterly seeing but not of feeling. In the reshaping of her art, which was soon to commence, her religious and spiritual attitudes would play an important part.

Although Carr had rebelled against the "large, furious helps"[1] in which religion was served up at home, she continued to attend church long after she was freed of family authority. Religion, however, was more than a habit for Carr; it was an innate attitude and came to have an important bearing on her art. The first link between her art and religion was forged in November 1927 when she first met Lawren Harris and others of the Group of Seven and their circle. That date also marks the beginning of her Journals in which she writes about her spiritual life at some length, and of the decisive change in direction that her life and work took.

On first seeing the painting of these eastern Canadian artists she was rapturous: "If I could pray, if I knew where to find a god to pray to, I would pray, 'God bless the Group of Seven,'"[2] a statement that shows she had not yet found a belief to answer her adult needs. She felt at once that she might find God in their work — "the God I've longed and hunted for and failed to find."[3] Harris, the Group's intellectual and theorist, was a committed theosophist, and his artistic ideas and attitudes grew in large measure out of his theosophic beliefs. The quality Carr found in Harris's painting, "rising into serene, uplifted places, above the swirl into holy places,"[4] she identified as religious, and knew at once that his religion and his painting were one. Although the Group's work as a whole assumed a relationship between art and religion, Carr found his language clearer than that of the others; on his recommendation she promptly purchased a copy of *Tertium Organum* by Ouspensky and prepared to delve into theosophy, if that was what gave his work "that something." She failed to anticipate the faithless, speculative nature of theosophy or to recognize the fact that though it postulated a supreme essence or principle, it was not a religion, certainly not in the sense of worshipful belief in a divine being.

Thus began her three-year struggle[5] to make her way through the complexities of theosophical doctrine and to reconcile its teachings with her long-established Christian beliefs. She did not find theosophical literature easy or sympathetic, but she had helpful discussions with Harris on two visits in Toronto, and with F.B. Housser and his wife Bess (later to become Mrs. Harris), who were also theosophists closely associated with the Group of Seven. Most important were Harris's letters to her, an intense exchange of correspondence carried on between 1928 and 1934, in which he responded to her questionings, encouraging her with simplified statements of various doctrines, and of his artistic and philosophic stances into which those doctrines had been assimilated. Certainly many of her general notions concerning the artist and the

QUEEN CHARLOTTE ISLANDS
TOTEM
watercolour 31

individual, as she reveals in the Journals, are reflections of Harris's beliefs and so are consistent with theosophical teachings. Among these, constantly reiterated in her writing and witnessed in her painting, is the belief in the central role of nature for the artist, and the idea that an artist's work should grow out of a prolonged attachment to a place and an absorption of its underlying character — the very "trees, skies, earth and rock of our own place" referred to by Harris in a letter to her in 1930.

She also believed that art must cast out the personal. "This I know, I shall not find it until it comes out of my inner self, until the God quality in me is in tune with the God in it. . . . until I have learned and fully realize my relationship to the Infinite."[6] Such a thought finds its counterpart in several of Harris's letters, such as the statement: "The soul has a different life from the personality — it alone is affected by . . . the spirit that informs nature."[7] And Carr believed in the continuity and interrelatedness of all existence; that life is ongoing and not an accomplishment, which is another view Harris shared with her on more than one occasion.

These and other ideas that Harris and Carr came to hold in common are not exclusive to theosophy, which represents a synthesis of philosophic and religious thought from various sources. Probably Harris simply helped her to formulate her beliefs to some degree and confirmed those she already held. But the parallels between their beliefs are too many, and her personal ties to him at that time too strong, not to conclude that essentially his thought became her own. She was not an analytical person and though she needed precepts to live and work by, she was not interested in their sources (any more than in the sources of her art), or aware of the steps by which she arrived at them. For the most part she simply gives voice to them in her writing as if they were her own.

There is, of course, no question of her failing to acknowledge the overall importance of Harris in her life, especially in those early years of their friendship when in his letters he opened to her "the rich cupboards of his heart, stored with art knowledge . . . riched with his own perception, his inner struggles, his bigness, . . . his hopes and high aims."[8]

Probably the most central and formative notion conveyed to her through this exchange was his investment of art with spiritual value and moral purpose, and his firm belief that art is an endeavour worthy of man's loftiest aspirations. Carr needed this elevated view of art to activate her latent strengths and to harness her great artistic and spiritual drives. But apart from this long-range gain, it is clear from several remarks in the Journals, and the sequence of those remarks, that she saw a relation between her involvement with theosophy and her coincident highly designed and conceptualized paintings of 1928-30/31, and similarly between the growing freedom in her work and her final break with theosophy. She reveals that relationship in an observation she made on a sketching trip in September 1934, when her theosophic association had ended: "Form is fine, and colour and design and subject matter but that which does not speak to the heart is worthless. It is the intensity of feeling you have about a thing that counts. . . . When I tried to see things theosophically I was looking through the glasses of cold, hard, inevitable fate, serene perhaps but cold, unjoyous and unmoving. Seeing things the Christ way, things are dipped in love. It warms and humanizes them. . . . God as cold, inexorable law is terrible. God as love is joyous."[9]

The connection between theosophy and Carr's conceptualized paintings was primarily derived from Harris's work, which at that time was also very disciplined and formalized, and he was, in his letters, encouraging her in that direction. But it was also probably to some degree more directly the result of her effort to see her painting "through theosophy"[10] — through a set of beliefs based on clear theory and explication that would call for thoughtfulness, clarity and definition in artistic expression.

In any case, however much theosophy she was able to absorb and utilize for its practical

32

34

33

and emotional help and as a support for her artistic stance, as a religious doctrine she found it wanting. While in a troubled state, she sought help from her theosophic friends on a last visit to Toronto in the fall of 1933 and was momentarily satisfied, finding that "they [chiefly Lawren, Bess, Fred] escape into a bigger realm and lose themselves in the divine whole. To make God personal is to make him little, finite, not infinite. I want the big God."[11] But the bolstering did not last. The theoretical nature of theosophy was clearly irreconcilable with the lessons of experience in her own life. Her religious requirement included a "real God, not the distant, mechanical, theosophical one"[12]; a personal God to whom she could pray and who would speak to her. The presence of God runs through the Journals like a supra-human father: divine but real.

And so Carr decided to go her own way. After attending a series of lectures by Raja Singh, a Christian Hindu and associate of Mahatma Ghandi, whose "child-like, simple faith — no sect, no creed, no bonds but just God and Christ"[13] touched her deeply, she wrote Harris in December 1933, telling him she could not swallow some of the theosophy ideas, and in January 1934 she wrote again, "snapping the theosophy bond."[14] She was afraid that this might end the sustaining association she had enjoyed with him and others in eastern Canada, in which support for her art and help in her spiritual quest had been so intertwined. Doubtless this fear had kept her struggle with theosophy going for so long. She need not have worried that Harris would end the friendship because of her return to Christianity, but the vital period of their relationship had ended, chiefly because her own strength and confidence had increased her independence.

The poetry of Walt Whitman, to which Fred Housser had introduced her, was also important in the evolution of Carr's view of the world. His *Leaves of Grass* and other volumes were daily reading companions to the end of her life. In his dithyrambic and rolling song she found a powerful echo in which she could "hear" herself, for like her own mature work, Whitman's poetry postulated a passionate and restless self that was both the exuberant centre of, and yet an insignificant atom in the universe.

In 1940 she was to comment on her religious evolution: "I *am* religious and I always have been. But I am not a church-goer and my attitude towards the Bishop, whose narrow church views I could not accept, made my family's disgust of me . . . pronounce me irreligious and wicked. . . . Alone, I crept into many strange churches of different denominations, in San Francisco, in London, in Indian villages way up north, and was comforted by the solemnity. But at home, bribed occasionally into the Reformed Episcopal, I sat fuming at the mournful, 'We beseech Thee to hear us, Good Lord.' . . . I longed to get out of church and crisp up in the open air. God got so stuffy squeezed into a church. Only out in the open was there room for Him. He was like a great breathing among the trees. In church he was static, a bearded image in petticoats. In the open He had no form; He just *was*, and filled all the universe."[15] In the long run Carr had to find God for herself, and that she did, without benefit of creed, in a pantheism suited to her own simplicity. In nature He "filled all the universe."

IMPORTANT INFLUENCES: HARRIS AND TOBEY   What Carr drew from the Group of Seven was the inspiration of their militant Canadianism and their great sense of purpose. Harris was part of that general inspiration, and his work struck with especial force. "I have never felt anything like the power of those canvases. They seem to have called to me from some other world, sort of an answer to a great longing."[16] His *Above Lake Superior*, which she had probably already read about in Housser's book, moved her deeply as did his mountain paintings. Then there was the sea painting that she saw in his house and which she subsequently described in her Journal in such detail as to leave no doubt of its effect on her: "A heavenly light lay upon one corner, shining

peacefully. Three cloud forms, almost straight shafts with light on their tips, pointed to it. Across a blue-green sky, a long, queer cloud lay lower down, almost on the horizon, but you could move in and on and beyond it. A small purplish round island, then four long, simple rock forms, purple-brown, with the blue sea lapping them. Two warmer green earth forms and some quiet grey forms that might be tree trunks in the foreground. Peace. My spirit entered the quiet spaces of the picture."[17]

By the time Carr met him, Harris had abandoned the flatness, the heavy pigmentation and the decorative elements of his earlier painting and was moving towards a more metaphysical art. As the locations for his paintings became more remote and austere — bare trees, frozen lakes, mountains, glaciers — so his form assumed an appropriate equivalence: reduced colour range with increasing emphasis on the non-sensory blues and greens relating to distant space; suppression of detail or surface interruption in favour of smoothly delineated and modelled — and idealized — forms; light pervading the space of the picture or formalized into directional shafts, either device implying a symbolic presence.

Both Harris's concept of painting as reflecting metaphysical-spiritual states of being and his specific pictorial devices were to have a strong influence on Carr over the next couple of years. In an undated letter, probably written in the fall of 1929, he stressed the importance of design to her: "You can in one sense, in one part of you, forget the spirit — it is innate in you — but push the forms to the limit in volume, plasticity, and precision and relationships in one unified, functioning greater form which is the picture . . . the last picture you sent me shows a greater concern for precision of design but the form could be intensified, given even more power." [18] One of the books he recommended to her in Toronto was Clive Bell's *Art* in which Bell propounds his theory of significant form, and this would have confirmed Harris's advice.

Carr was also receiving advice from the American artist Mark Tobey, who had first come to Seattle in 1922. He taught there for a while and sometime between then and mid-1925 he spent a week in her Victoria studio. Very likely he was the American artist who advised her that her beds, dishes and meals would wait, "young morning on Beacon Hill won't. Don't tether yourself to a dishpan, woman! Beds, vegetables! They are not the essentials!"[19]

A bright and engaging young artist almost twenty years Carr's junior, Tobey was on friendly terms with a small group of artist acquaintances from Seattle who stayed with her from time to time in the twenties. And in the fall of 1928, after returning from several years of travel, he gave a three-week advanced course in her studio. She wrote enthusiastically about these classes to Eric Brown: "I had just got straightened [from her summer trip to northern Indian villages] when 'Mr. Tobey' an American artist came over from the states for three weeks. He was on his way to Chicago where he is to give an exhibition of his paintings. He is a man that interests me very much, very modern and very keen . . . I think he is one of the best teachers I know of. He gave a short course of classes here in my studio, and I felt I got a tremendous lot of help from his criticisms. He was very keen on my summer's work and his crits, I feel, will be very useful in the working out of many problems connected with my summer's work which I hope to do this winter."[20] He stayed in her studio in the spring of 1930 when she went to Toronto and to New York, and in November of that year, obviously feeling that she could still use his help, she sent him five dollars to come and give her a criticism. He did not come but kept the five dollars — which angered her — and instead sent a letter with advice. She recorded in her Journals that he had told her she would have to "pep my work up and get off the monotone, even exaggerate light and shade, to watch rhythmic relations and reversals of detail, to make my canvases two thirds half-tone, one third black and white. Well, it sounds good but it's rather painting to recipe, isn't it? I know I am in a monotone. My forests are too monotonous. I must pep them up

THE GREAT EAGLE, SKIDEGATE B.C.
watercolour 36

with higher contrasts. But what is it all without soul? It's dead. It's the hole you put the thing into, the space that wraps it round, and the God in the thing that counts above everything. Still, he's right too. I must pep up."[21]

Tobey at that time already had a vision of a free and vitalistic form, though his ideas were ahead of his art which was still immature and moving in several directions at once. He was said to be an effective and non-academic teacher but authoritarian,[22] forcing on his students whatever ideas had captured him at the time. Carr found it difficult to learn from someone with whom she was not in personal sympathy, but she conceded that he was a better teacher than Harris. There are two kinds of effective teachers: those who inspire and create an ambience of thrilling possibility, and those who offer specific how-to-do-it help. Harris was certainly the former, Tobey more likely the latter. On the basis of Tobey's work it seems evident that his influence on her was not through his own painting but as a result of his painting theories and his specific comments on technical and formal matters.

Nearly thirty years later Colin Graham, who as Director of the Art Gallery of Greater Victoria was in touch with Tobey over many years, described Tobey's struggles with Carr. "He [Tobey] had evolved a system of volumetric analysis of forms combined with what he called the pressure of light areas against dark and vice versa. The latter he had derived from the work of El Greco while the former, as I understand it, was a form of analytical cubism. He described Emily as still heavily entrenched behind the buttresses of Impressionism and its offshoots and it was only after prolonged resistance that she came to him one day and said 'you win.'"[23]

That same year, 1957, when visiting Victoria, Tobey was to claim credit for Carr's acquiring an authoritative style. "She could not have developed to conceive the great swirling canvases, the wonderful tree forms, unless there had been someone to indicate the way for her. I was that someone."[24] This seems a large claim to be made almost thirty years later and on the basis of a limited encounter with her. She had been profoundly affected by Harris's work and had already started to find a direction through his northern paintings of the late twenties when, in September 1928, Tobey gave his classes. Yet, though the latter's open and specific criticisms were hard to take, she did write that letter asking for more; clearly he was of help to her. The answer to what he gave her may well lie in his words of recollection: those "great swirling canvases." Perhaps it was from him that she got the clue to the swirling, expansive factor in her form which was to become an animating character in her work from this time, something that Harris's ethereal spaces could not provide.

LAST INDIAN TRIPS   In the summer of 1928 Carr made a second and last trip up the Nass and Skeena rivers and again visited the Queen Charlotte Islands. A vivid letter to Eric Brown from South Bay, Skidegate, dated 11 August, describes the deteriorated state of the poles since her earlier visit as well as the hardships that she endured in travel, accommodation, weather and a nearly fatal boat trip during a storm. Despite the difficulties, she got about thirty large watercolours as well as many notes and drawings. In 1929 she visited Friendly Cove and in 1930, Quatsino — less arduous excursions to places nearer home.

At first sight many of these watercolours are almost indistinguishable from those of the 1912 trip showing some of the same locations — and understandably so, for the primary purpose was the same: to gather information. In any case, the Indian subjects had their own powerful identity, and Carr felt compelled to depict them with respect and fidelity. The handling of paintings like *Maud Island Q.C.I.*, *Queen Charlotte Islands Totem* or *South Bay, Skidegate* confirms this intent. There is, all the same, a subtle shift in her way of seeing the material. The featured forms are larger in relation to the picture space. The totem pole, a difficult form to handle pictorially, tends to be cut off more often and presented as a substantial mass, or it is supported from behind with a more solid screen of forest. In several watercolours of the village of Kispiox, poles overlap each other densely, in contrast to those of sixteen years earlier which often stood, needle-like, in open space. The result is a greater formal coherence and also a new dramatic expression.

There are other watercolours of 1928-29 which obviously were not done on location but were worked out in the studio. Possibly they were intended as intermediaries between on-the-spot information sketches and canvases, for Carr was entering a highly conceptualized and formalized phase of her work. *Great Eagle, Kitwancool* and an untitled totem pole with stylized trees show her working out a new formalized solution to the problem of depicting totem poles and their settings. In all of them a strong basis of drawing, searching out and establishing the form, underlies the watercolour, and confirms the exploratory nature of the works. In *Kitwancool* she had found a kind of formal simplification which can translate the poles, houses and nature forms so that they are part of a unified structure. Again, in *Great Eagle* the drama of the great bird thrusting against the upper margin is consistent in feeling with the dynamically abstracted planes of sky. *Indian Church, Friendly Cove* of 1929 (which relates to the famous canvas) and *Koskimo* of 1930 both have an immediacy and freedom which suggest that they were done on location. At the same time, the formalized and abstracted handling of foliage, as well as the bold compositional statements, indicate that her change to a conceptual vision, so carefully worked out and manifest in paintings of the year previous (such as the two watercolours mentioned above, or canvases like *Kitwancool*), has now been assimilated into her perception.

The speed with which Carr was learning, experimenting and producing works of increasing authority at this time, however stylistically derived, shows how much her artistry was at her command, even though it had been little exercised over the previous fifteen years.

Facsimile of opening paragraph of letter from Emily Carr to Eric Brown

First I went up the Skeena. I found the poles greatly deteriorated in the last 15 years. The restored ones have lost so much of interest and subtlety in the process. I appreciate the difficulties of restoring them, and it is certainly better to do it than let them utterly disappear, as they must have in a few years, but that heavy load of all over paint drowns them. I wish they would put on the preservatives and leave the colour, not soak the whole pole in grey paint. I met Mr. Campbell coming down the Skeena and we had some long talks. I fully appreciate the difficulties, but there is too much catering to the 'beastly tourist.' Things have to be made so blatant to please them, and the subtle beauty disappears. I had the luck to get into Kitwancool. I tried to 15 years ago but the white people would not let me as the Indians there are peculiar and resent white in intrusion greatly. A few months ago there was more trouble; they threatened the surveyors with axes. However, I went in on a waggon with the chief and his son and was very well treated. It is an *awful* waggon road — took 7 hours and nearly bumped the life out of me. The heat and dust were terrific. There were 4 Indian men (one just returning from jail). I went in for ten days and got held up for 5 by a terrific storm; it poured rain and hail for 4 days which made working *very difficult*. I crawled into little grave houses which were clammy, cold and leaky and always in the wrong spot to get the right view. I was particularly sorry not to do some better stuff there as the poles are very lovely. They are in shocking repair but the carving is so tenderly done, with great expression. I slept out the first night, but after the storm the Indians gave me a corner of their house. It was a huge log affair, very clean — just one enormous room. The chief and his wife and son had one corner, a married daughter, her husband and 3 children another, and I had mine. Was given a table and a chair and I had my own bed and hung my tent fly across the corner. While the weather stormed, there were good fires and it was cosy and I was much interested in it all. They were a fine bunch — kind, clean and dignified. There were two babies hanging up from the rafters in cradles which everyone shoved as they passed and kept rocking. I was struck with the great resemblance of the women to the carved faces on the poles; they might have been family portraits and probably some were. I worked in a broken-down community house which gave scanty shelter and was shared by some dozen Indian horses, who took all the dry spots and left me the leaks. I shall get some stuff out of my sketches but do wish I'd had fair weather. The mosquitoes up the river were *simply fearful*, work was a torment and it was not till I was fearfully bitten that I realized I *must* do something. It is all very well for the camera man: he gets things quickly. But to sit hour after hour and be eaten alive is fearful. All the Indians sleep with nets. I constructed a costume, however, consisting of a sack over my head with a small panel of glass let in the front to see through. I had two pairs of gloves, one over the other, one kid, and they bit through *both* pair and a pair of heavy canvas pantalettes that hung loose down to the soles of my shoes. I was some beauty but managed to work. Was two weeks on the Skeena during which time I had only one really *fine* day (tho' before that it was very hot and I believe it was after). Then I went up the Nass. The fish went with me, and from the day I got there the cannery and boats were very busy and the mosquitoes were also. I had to stick round the cannery most of the time but got away for a week to 'Grenville' and lived in an empty school house back in a mosquito swamp. Every soul in the village was away except one man and woman who live a long way from my school house. This man took me to the other villages in his own boat. He had lumbago and one eye and was very lame, so all the packing fell on me. It was in this village I was particularly glad of the company of my wee dog, 'Ginger Pop.' He is a tiny chap — six lbs. — but he is very brave, and he's ruled all the Indian dogs out of their own villages with the air of an aristocrat. The Indians think he is wonderful, and he has been great company in spooky places and no trouble. The Indians go to the canneries and leave their dogs in the villages half starving. I used to share my food with the poor brutes, and when I *carried* (Ginger Pop) my own little dog, six or seven gaunt dogs padded after me everywhere. We became great pals and it greaved [sic] me to leave them on the wharf, craning their scraggy necks over and looking with such beseeching eyes. After returning to Prince Rupert and sorting up my pack, I came on to Queen Charlotte Islands here. I expected to get my best work and was very keen. I got to two villages and did quite a bit; then it has rained *incessantly* ever since I came. Last Wednesday I contracted with an Indian who had a gas boat to take me to three villages way off over bad waters. It was supposed to be a good boat, and we got to the first village 'Skedans.' I had been sick and got them to land me the first moment (amid *pouring* rain); the man, his son and daughter went back to the boat to have their dinner and suddenly a great storm came up. They got the girl on shore, but the man and boy had a *fearful time*; the boat was drifting fearfully, the engine would not work and the anchors were fouled with the thick sea weed. She had drifted so far they had a long, long way to row — it was just awful watching. Time and time again the boat disappeared altogether. They never expected to make it, nor I to see them land. My little dog was left behind on the big boat which was starting drifting on to the rocks. We scratched up some kind of a meal and prepared to spend the night on the beach in the pouring rain. It was a wild spot — quite a few totems, dense undergrowth. I would have enjoyed it, I was so thankful the man and boy had not been drowned in front of our eyes, for with the tangle of kelp they could not have swam and the waves were *terrific*, but to see the boat banging to pieces with my poor pup on board was horrible. Just as it got dark a seine fishing boat caught our distress signals and came. I was glad to see the boat saved, but how I did hate going out on that awful sea. It was a party of Norwegians. They got our boat off the rocks and towed her behind, but we went on the big boat — oooooooh, I *was* sick. I lay flat on my back on the top of the fish hatch and did not care what happened — didn't know where we were going and don't know yet. We banged round for hours, and the captain gave me his cabin, and eventually we were landed in Cumshewa Inlet on a fish scow. The Indians slept on their damaged boat and I was given a Japanese fish boat's Captain's cabin — and turned out at 4.a.m. when she went out. The two men on the scow had a tiny cabin and fed Ginger Pop and myself royally. Next day a fish packer came in and, as they were eventually going to South Bay, took me along. It was quite a hot time but the part that makes me sore is that I did not get to those other two villages. I'd contracted with the Indian for $50 for a 4-day trip. I had $50 worth of experiences but, oh, I *did want my work*. Travel round these Islands really is terrific. Well, I should be thankful I have my life, for if the engine had gone bad before we got to land in that awful sea we'd have all been lost, and in spite of everything I have quite a bunch of work to keep me busy this winter from my sketches. Rain seems to have followed me everywhere. . . .

M Emily Carr

A FORMAL PERIOD

A POSTCUBIST REFERENCE   The three years between 1928 and 1931 were productive ones for Carr. Then, in solemnly heavy canvases of the forest and of big Indian poles in various settings, she showed herself to be an artist of major power. She left behind the painterly approach she had used since her French sojourn and now translated what she saw in nature into simplified, solid, three-dimensional pictorial forms which she detached optically from the canvas surface and placed in deep space. The work is the most formal and the most designed of her career and, with the exception of the fauvist-derived paintings, the most marked by identifiable outside influence. Yet the paintings are unmistakably her own and among them are some of the most indelible images of her entire output. This was also the period of her closest association with Harris and his strongest influence on her thought and her art; of her theosophic struggles; of Mark Tobey's impact; and of her introduction to Walt Whitman's writings.

Two undated paintings, *The Crying Totem* and *Skidegate* (nos. 39 and 40) may represent the modest beginnings of this symbolic phase of Carr's work — early efforts made in the first half of 1928 to infuse into her painting what she had seen in the East. They relate in a number of ways to 1912 paintings, for instance *Skidegate* (no 40), in format and in the handling of background or foreground as decorative backdrop; but significantly, in the 1928 paintings the tachist intent is gone, and the colour, which now belongs to the depicted forms and not to the brush strokes, is almost a monochrome. In the later *Skidegate* the leafless, vertical tree spars are close to being pure Harris.

This period of highly conceptualized works includes a small group of stylized paintings in which a dynamic geometry is introduced into scenes, usually of totems in open village settings. The geometry is arbitrary in that it does not derive, analytically or descriptively, from the forms depicted. And ultimately it is of cubist reference, just as the Orphism or Futurism, which certain of her works more immediately recall, also find their origins in Cubism. This group (as well as the several watercolours previously discussed) includes *Kitwancool*, the canvas in the Glenbow-Alberta Institute, *Kispiax Village*, in the Art Gallery of Ontario, *The Raven*, from a private collection, and *Big Raven* and *British Columbia Indian Village*, in the Vancouver Art Gallery. In these paintings, land forms are restructured as a series of interweaving planes, and pendant clouds and light shafts are given volume and density by deep modelling and tonal contrast. Forms thrust, spring, expand or retract forcefully; there are taut curves of short radius, dilating cubes, weighted diagonals, and clearly delineated contours.

Carr's position in relation to the postcubist vein in twentieth-century art parallels her previous relation to Postimpressionism. When she was working in the area of postimpressionist colour and form, her natural inclination had been towards its expressionist possibilities, as was that of the Fauves. Now, in making use of a postcubist idiom, her natural affinity was towards its dynamic-futurist extension and its potential for expressing motion and energy. The inferred influence is that of such artists as Delaunay, Franz Marc or other Europeans who, almost twenty years before, had been redirecting the cubist discovery of broken form to their own less formalist goals. The direct influence had to be closer to home. Harris in the late twenties was painting formalized skies with directional shafts of light; Tobey had made his "own personal discovery of cubism,"[1] a highly illuminating insight into that movement but not the explanation usually provided by art historians. A canvas he painted in 1928, *Emily Carr's Studio*, involves a principle of dislocated planes and discontinuity of space that she never practised. Neither of these influences, particularly that of Tobey, seems adequate to account fully for this cubist-based element in her painting. Indeed, her canvas *Kitwancool*, probably painted in the spring of 1928, predates Tobey's classes in her studio.

She may have seen other more closely cubist-derived work than that of Harris or Tobey

on her short but momentous eastern visit at the end of 1927. A particularly suggestive analogy is presented by the symbolic abstractions of fellow-Canadian Bertram Brooker during the years 1927-30, works that declared their spiritual intent in such romantic-epic titles as *Endless Dawn, The Way, The Dawn of Man*. His painting was among the earliest abstract work done in Canada, and though Carr could not have seen his solo exhibition in Toronto, which was held in January 1927, he was a friend of Harris and others of the Toronto circle, and her visits might have given her an opportunity to see some of his work. She could have seen his painting again on her trip to Toronto and New York in the spring of 1930. He, for his part, included her 1928 painting *Kitwancool Totems* in his *Yearbook of the Arts in Canada* for 1928-29. *Kitwancool* is an interesting if unsuccessful canvas; its somewhat tentative nature and its failure to find an integration between the poles and their formalized setting suggests that it was an early experiment. If, as information on the back of the painting indicates, it was painted in the spring of 1928, then it was done before her first visit to Kitwancool that summer. She probably worked it out from a photograph when she was excitedly anticipating her journey north. A photographic source might also in this case help explain the uncertain handling of the poles, which lack the impressive volumetric assurance of subsequent canvases.

Other paintings in the same vein achieve a more successful formal fusion as well as expressive statement. In *The Raven*, the simple planes of the bird on its pole are echoed by shallowly curving flat planes of sky, giving the painting a monumental structure. This echoing sky also suggests nature's capacity for expressing human sympathy, a sentiment that Carr occasionally allows to creep into her paintings — sometimes to their detriment.

The cubist vision, even in the vastly modified form in which she applied it, was never for her an understood attitude or theory, nor even a whole view which left a consistent imprint in the painting. She uses the cubist approach most consistently in the Kitwancool watercolour and in several charcoal forest studies. In *Big Raven* and *Vanquished* the cubist element belongs only to the active and highly structured skies; the swirling, viscous green jungle and the solid wood bird and poles belong to different categories both of nature and of form, though she has successfully unified all the components within a larger overall dynamic character. These two canvases, completed some three years later than *Kitwancool*, also point out how she employed the cubist idea in the developing expressiveness of her own art, using it not as a form-fragmenting process but as a structuring one, with expressive rather than analytical intent. Light, and sky the transmitter of light, were from now on to constitute a major element in her expressive equipment, which she would learn to handle in other ways. Here, too, one can observe a mannerism, also of cubist inference, that of back-lighting around contours, which serves to delineate form as well as to create an expressive aura.

The cubist-derived manner of handling foliage that Carr used in 1929 canvases like *Indian Church* aimed at simplification, consolidation, and the creation of mass rather than at its fracturing or dissolution. Her concern was not so much to formalize the material as to find an equivalent form for the dark and enclosing forest experience with which she was at that time preoccupied. In these few years, when she was making up for lost time and engaging in energetic experimentation, she worked in several modes in rapid succession, and sometimes simultaneously.

USE OF PHOTOGRAPHS "You must be absolutely honest in the depicting of a totem for meaning is attached to every line. You must be most particular about detail and proportion. I never use the camera nor work from photos; every pole in my collection has been studied from its own actual reality in its own original setting, and

38

39

40

I have as you might term it, been personally acquainted with every pole here shown. Indians I think express it well when they say to one another 'come and see the woman make pictures with her head and hands, not with a box' . . . though they have seen them and some use them."2 The insistence of this statement from Carr's talk for her 1913 exhibition of Indian paintings in Vancouver, suggests the stricture against the use of photographic aids in painting which was prevalent at the time, and also her own stand on the matter. There are three photos in the British Columbia Provincial Museum in Victoria showing Carr at her easel in northern Indian village sites. In the lecture on totem poles quoted above she speaks of a young Canadian girl who accompanied her from Skidegate to Chaatl, and it was probably she, or another companion, who took these snapshots on Carr's 1912 visit to the Queen Charlotte Islands. Theoretically these photographs could have been used to confirm or amplify her information when she was painting at home.

Certainly by 1928 Carr had sufficiently lifted the taboo to permit herself the use of photographs, although this was not a subject she discussed openly. The likelihood of the canvas *Kitwancool* having been developed from a photographic source has already been mentioned, and the fact that *Blunden Harbour* certainly was has been documented elsewhere.3 The case for *Heina* in the National Gallery's collection also seems clear. With the exception of Masset and Skidegate the old Haida villages were abandoned by the turn of the century, and Carr could not have seen the village as she depicted it in this 1928 canvas. A photograph taken by Maynard in 1884 is the source from which she executed a handsome watercolour-drawing, and then the canvas. A similar source for *Totem Village,* in the Vancouver Art Gallery collection, a painting that closely resembles *Heina* in style, is indicated by two unfinished pencil drawings in the Provincial Archives of British Columbia in Victoria, which are inscribed in an unidentified hand, possibly that of Willie Newcombe, as "unfinished sketch from photograph."

A NEW UNDERSTANDING OF THE INDIAN'S ART   Brooding silence is the mood, and formalization the mode, in Carr's 1928-30 canvases of coastal totem poles set against rain forests — canvases such as *Nirvana, Potlatch Welcome, Guyasdoms' D'Sonoqua, Old Time Coast Village.* Later on, when she was working with greater freedom and spontaneity, Carr was to think back to these strongly formalized paintings, recognize their degree of dependence on outside sources, and find them too designed. Yet the cohesive world that she was painting at this time, with its weight, solidity and density, was becoming increasingly her own creation. These canvases rely for their basic character on an architectonic, vertical structure of poles or tree trunks interconnected laterally with the volumetric curves and spirals of foliage, and spatially with clearly stated relationships between overlapping or receding planes.
The way the poles are presented in these paintings, as compared to that in her earlier ones, shows that Carr is now working from the expressive power of the Indian's art. She has discovered the profound relationship between the Indian's mythology as expressed in his carvings and the oppressive character of the powerful natural environment to which those carvings belong, and of which they speak. These poles are often dealt with singly and enlarged in scale so that they fill much of the picture area with their towering, looming, sometimes precariously leaning presences. Whereas her 1912 paintings of the same subjects often displayed a wide expanse of open sky, in these canvases space tends to be claustrophobically limited, sometimes by crowding large, overlapping masses, as in *Three Totems,* or by bringing forest or other backdrops close into the picture plane. At other times she uses the forest background in such a way as to suggest, metaphorically, its underlying relationship to the Indian's art. *Totem and Forest* seems to be an almost explicit statement of that relationship, though she

41

42

43

44

might not have seen this particular pole in its original setting. The exceptionally narrow vertical format echoes the tree trunk form and suggests the confinement of dense woods. Compositionally it is then divided into three additional totem-like vertical strips: two of forest, the third the pole itself. Spatially the three totemic strips exist in one shallow plane and their likeness is further established by the reduction of tone and colour contrasts. The painting reveals Carr's insight that the Indian has carved into his totem pole the same silences, tensions, orifices, secrecies as nature has in her forests. *Indian Church*, one of her best-known paintings, similarly employs a symmetrical, shallow-spaced composition with forest matrix and church facade facing the viewer in timeless confrontation, but here the contrast of alien white seems to suggest the intrusion of man into nature's domain.

SHIFT TO THE FORESTS   "I'm still on Indian stuff as it's too wet for the woods," Carr wrote at the end of March 1931, which suggests that in her mind she had already moved into the woods. Around 1930-31 the Indian themes ceased to be a major preoccupation, though she returned to them from time to time in individual canvases, particularly in later years. Lawren Harris no doubt played a part in this decision, for in a letter undated but probably sent in the late fall of 1929, he suggested that she leave them alone for a year or more because "the totem pole is a work of art in its own right and it is very difficult to use it in another form of art. But how about seeking an equivalent for it in the exotic landscape of the Island and coast, making your own form and forms within the greater form. Create new things from the landscape, houses, steps, beaches and what not."[5] Mark Tobey also gave her similar advice to leave the Indians and poles and to paint from inside herself. Probably these suggestions only strengthened her own inclination, for the totem poles, in taking her deeper — literally and figuratively — into the primeval woods, had revealed to her a more comprehensive world: a nature vast and rich enough to provide her with pictorial metaphors for all the experiences she would wish to express. Such paintings as *Totem and Forest*, *Indian Church* and *Old Time Coast Village* already foretell such a move in their thematic balance between forest and Indian, and they were done at the same time as a handsome series, including *Western Forest*, *Inside a Forest* and others, in which the forest itself is explored.

Her formulae for handling forest and undergrowth vary from cubistically cut and chiselled shapes to moulded and overlapping plastic slabs of green to swirling heavy streams and ropes of growth, but they all belong to a concept of nature that is, at this time, still, silent, mysterious and often forbidding. Carr sometimes conceives of the forest as an impenetrable space-consuming wall, shutting out light and sky, or as shadowed interior, and at times she ascribes to the forest the sense of terrible presence she had found in the totem.

One such painting is the dramatic *Forest, British Columbia*. Composition and space are stage-like; passages between the ancient grey-brown tree trunks lead off to wings left and right; great curtains of heavy foliage hang and float in weighted turgid rhythms through which a shaft of grey light enters the dark interior. As elsewhere in her work, light is assigned its primal symbolic role of dispelling dark and creating life, and the resulting dramatic sense of waiting, watching and foreboding is intense. Another work of this genre is *Grey*, one of the most remarkable paintings of Carr's career. The theme of a young tree in the company of its elders recurs in other paintings and sketches such as *The Little Pine* and *A Young Tree* and the 1932 oil-on-paper *Forest Interior*. In paintings on this theme it is usually the vitality of the young tree that is being celebrated, expressed by its strategic positioning in the composition, its brighter colour, more active rhythms and so on, in contrast with the more sober growth around it. But the young tree of *Grey* belongs to a nature that is metaphysical rather than material, and

Skedans on a stormy day looked menacing. To the right of the Bay
immediately behind the reef, rose a pair of uncouth cone-like hills,
their heads bonneted in lowering clouds. The clumsy hills were
heavily treed save where deep bare scars ran down their sides.
. . . Wind raced across the breast-high growth around the meagre
ruins more poignantly desolate for having once known man.

A row of crazily tipped totem poles straggled along the low bank
skirting Skedans Bay. The poles were deep planted to defy storms.
In their bleached and hollow upper ends stood coffin-boxes boarded
endwise into the pole by heavy cedar planks boldly carved with
the crest of the little huddle of bones inside the box, bones which
had once been a chief of Eagle, Bear or Whale Clan.

Klee Wyck, pp. 80-81

the role it plays is that of silent watching rather than released energy. In its restricted palette this canvas relates to another group of works: oil-on-paper or oil-on-card sketches of deep forest which are carried out in a near-monochrome of blacks and greys but with a great deal of tonal contrast. Possibly these were experimental responses to Tobey's advice "to get off the monotone."

Grey, however, is in a class by itself, being at the same time the most formal and the most poetic of her works. Here is the forest viewed in the night of our imagining, inviting yet fearful. It is forest pictured from the edge outside (the path on the right luring us in and the dark tree forms visible in profile against a pearly sky in the upper left), yet simultaneously experienced as though from inside at the centre. It is the forest presented as a night chrysalis, sliced through its enfolding and overlapping layers to reveal its delicate core. A faintly tinted incandescence, self-generated, like that from a cooling fire, glows from the opening in the central conical tree, which is also an eye or a mouth or a womb, while an external light falls gently on the frontal planes exposed to our sight, giving the whole the character of a timeless vision mysteriously revealed out of the dark. Nowhere has Carr more powerfully suggested her mystical participation in the dark and fearsome spirit of the forest, for it is a dramatic statement made without the use of theatrical devices.

Grey might also be regarded as the ultimate tribute to Harris and the great spiritual debt she owed him. He had encouraged the design element in her work of which this canvas is the supreme statement. And in recommending that she leave the Indian theme he must have known that she could now carry forward the understanding of the whole symbolizing process of art she had learned while under the Indian spell. This painting is both the evidence of her debt and proof of her finally won independence. She was entering into her last great period of painting from the full range of her own resources.

CUMSHEWA
watercolour 47

BIG RAVEN
oil on canvas 48

Not far from the house sat a great wooden raven mounted on a rather low pole; his wings were flattened to his sides. A few feet from him stuck up an empty pole. His mate had sat there but she had rotted away long ago, leaving him moss-grown, dilapidated and alone to watch dead Indian bones, for these two great birds had been set, one on either side of the doorway of a big house that had been full of dead Indians who had died during a smallpox epidemic.

Klee Wyck, p. 21

. . . Cumshewa seems always to drip, always to be blurred with mist, its foliage always to hang wet-heavy. . . .

. . . these strong young trees . . . grew up round the dilapidated old raven, sheltering him from the tearing winds now that he was old and rotting because the rain seeped through the moss that grew upon his back and in the hollows of his eye-sockets. The Cumshewa totem poles were dark and colourless, the wood toneless from pouring rain. . . .

The memory of Cumshewa is of a great lonesomeness smothered in a blur of rain.

Klee Wyck, pp. 20, 21

KWAKIUTL
watercolour 49

POTLATCH FIGURE
oil on canvas 50

POTLATCH WELCOME
oil on canvas 51

49

50

KITWA[N]COOL TOTEMS
oil on canvas 52

TOTEM MOTHER, KITWANCOOL
oil on canvas 53

INDIAN HUT, QUEEN
CHARLOTTE ISLANDS
oil on canvas 54

53

54

The sun enriched the old poles grandly. They were carved elaborately
and with great sincerity. Several times the figure of a woman that
held a child was represented. The babies had faces like wise little
old men. The mothers expressed all womanhood — the big wooden
hands holding the child were so full of tenderness they had to be
distorted enormously in order to contain it all. Womanhood was
strong in Kitwancool.

Klee Wyck, p. 102

GUYASDOMS' D'SONOQUA
oil on canvas 55

Her head and trunk were carved out of, or rather into, the bole of
a great red cedar. She seemed to be part of the tree itself, as if she
had grown there at its heart, and the carver had only chipped away
the outer wood so that you could see her. Her arms were spliced
and socketed to the trunk, and were flung wide in a circling,
compelling movement. Her breasts were two eagle-heads, fiercely
carved. That much, and the column of her great neck, and her
strong chin, I had seen when I slithered to the ground beneath her.
Now I saw her face.

The eyes were two rounds of black, set in wider rounds of white,
and placed in deep sockets under wide, black eyebrows. Their fixed
stare bored into me as if the very life of the old cedar looked out,
and it seemed that the voice of the tree itself might have burst from
that great round cavity, with projecting lips, that was her mouth.
Her ears were round, and stuck out to catch all sounds. The salt
air had not dimmed the heavy red of her trunk and arms and thighs.
Her hands were black, with blunt finger-tips painted a dazzling
white. I stood looking at her for a long, long time.

Klee Wyck, p. 33

KOSKIMO
watercolour 56

Gumbooted and carrying Koko I clambered over the side — three
cats waited for me on the pebbly beach, ugly mottled lean yellow-
eyed beasts. The man and boat left, another cat joined me and a
speckled pullet — they crowded round my camp stool, quarrelling
who should get next to me after the first wary look. . . . I worked
all day . . . I left them meowing dolefully at the very edge of the sea.
Next day I went again. Before the engine stopped, before I was in
the row boat I heard them, not 4 but 8 running to the water's edge
and meowing like the Halleleulah chorus . . . I could scarcely walk
without treading on them. They meowed and rubbed ten times
harder than yesterday. . . . from 9 to 6 I worked and my court
surrounded me.

Unpublished journals, August-September 1930, Public Archives of Canada

56

ZUNOQUA OF THE CAT VILLAGE
oil on canvas 57

KOSKIMO
charcoal on paper 58

STRANGLED BY GROWTH
oil on canvas 59

I worked all afternoon, first on "Koskemo Village," X.1., and then on X.2, "Strangled by Growth," which is also Koskemo (the cat village). It is D'Sonoqua on the housepost up in the burnt part, strangled round by undergrowth. I want the pole vague and the tangle of growth strenuous. I want the ferocious, strangled lonesomeness of that place, creepy, nervy, forsaken, dank, dirty, dilapidated, the rank smell of nettles and rotting wood, the lush greens of the rank sea grass and the overgrown bushes, and the great dense forest behind full of unseen things and great silence, and on the sea the sun beating down, and on the sand, everywhere, circling me, that army of cats, purring and rubbing, following my every footstep. That was some place! There was a power behind it all, and stark reality.

Hundreds and Thousands, p. 26

58

59

She appeared to be neither wooden nor stationary, but a singing spirit, young and fresh, passing through the jungle. No violence coarsened her; no power domineered to wither her. She was graciously feminine. Across her forehead her creator had fashioned the Sistheutl, or mythical two-headed sea-serpent. One of its heads fell to either shoulder, hiding the stuck-out ears, and framing her face from a central parting on her forehead which seemed to increase its womanliness.

Klee Wyck, pp. 39-40

60

61

63

64

EMILY CARR

SOUTH BAY, SKIDEGATE
watercolour 66

OLD TIME COAST VILLAGE
oil on canvas 67

Untitled
oil on canvas 68

70

INDIAN CHURCH
oil on canvas 69

Untitled
oil on canvas, white gesso ground 70

INSIDE A FOREST II
oil on canvas 71

THE INDIAN CHURCH, FRIENDLY COVE
watercolour and charcoal on paper 72

72

71

73

74

98

OLD TREE AT DUSK
oil on canvas 76

FOREST, BRITISH COLUMBIA
oil on canvas 78

TREE
oil on canvas 77

OLD AND NEW FOREST
oil on canvas 79

THE LITTLE PINE
oil on canvas 80

SEA DRIFT AT THE EDGE OF THE
FOREST
oil on canvas 81

GREY
oil on canvas 82

79

80

81

WIDER CONTACTS/TECHNICAL CHANGES

Detail 84

A BROADER CONTEXT   The year 1928 marked Carr's return to full painting activity and also witnessed her increased participation in exhibitions of more than local significance. Such participation was increasingly on the basis of invitation, indicating that art officials were beginning to pay attention to her work. She exhibited with the Group of Seven in eastern Canada in 1930 and 1931; with its successor, the Canadian Group of Painters; and occasionally, with the Ontario Society of Artists exhibitions. She participated in a women's international exhibition in Detroit in 1929, and in exhibitions of Canadian art circulated by the National Gallery of Canada and shown in Washington, D.C., and other American cities during the early thirties. In 1930 she had an exhibition at the Art Institute of Seattle; in 1933 she was represented in an international exhibition of women artists in Amsterdam, and in 1937 she had paintings shown in London and Paris. In 1935 and 1937 she had solo shows in Toronto, the first at the Lyceum Club and Women's Art Association, the second at the University of Toronto's Hart House. She was by this time and would continue to be a well-established part of the larger Canadian art scene.

Untitled
charcoal 83

Untitled
charcoal on paper 84

Early in 1937, while in hospital suffering from the first of a number of heart attacks, Carr was visited by Eric Newton, then art critic for the *Manchester Guardian*, who was in Canada on a lecture tour. Since he was in western Canada, he had been asked by the National Gallery in Ottawa to visit her and to select some paintings for purchase in eastern Canada. He was enthusiastic about her work and from the group of fifteen he selected, three were purchased that spring by the National Gallery and three by the Art Gallery of Toronto. Others were bought by private collectors.

The home scene also improved after 1927. In 1930 she had an exhibition at Victoria's Crystal Garden which lasted several days, and she gave a talk to the sponsoring Women's Canadian Club. Despite the increased opportunities given her for exhibiting farther afield, the response of a close-range audience was clearly important to her, for she continued to show with the Island Arts and Crafts Society and periodically opened her Victoria studio to the public.

By the end of the twenties there were several artists of stature in the Vancouver community, among them F.H. Varley, J.W.G. Macdonald, Charles Scott and W.P. Weston, with whose work hers would share company in group exhibitions. By 1931 Vancouver had a civic art gallery, where she could show with the British Columbia Society of Fine Arts and in the Gallery's annual juried exhibitions. Her first solo show there in 1938 was well received. A letter to Eric Brown reveals that she was particularly pleased to have succeeded in making the spirit of western places speak to westerners, a reaction always more important to her than favourable reviews which discussed only technical matters. After that, almost every year until her death she had solo shows at the Vancouver Art Gallery. At that time artists could apply for space, paying a small rental fee, and Carr often referred to these shows as her "annuals."

The publication of *Klee Wyck* in 1941 (which won the Governor General's award for that year) and *The Book of Small* in the following year, brought her a kind of popular reputation that twenty years of painting had not done. Her biggest financial success from painting came with the exhibition of her work arranged by Dr. Max Stern for his Dominion Gallery in Montreal in 1944, which resulted in substantial sales.

This pattern of exhibiting, which commenced with the 1927 Ottawa show, continued through the thirties until her death, though after 1937 increasingly poor health curtailed her personal involvement in the mechanics of exhibiting as well as in painting itself. Throughout these years the strength and individuality of her work, even in places where it was little known, drew favourable critical attention from such serious reviewers as Eric Newton in England and G. Campbell McInnes in Toronto.

Despite the increased exposure that her paintings now enjoyed, despite the growing

recognition of her art and, towards the end, her increased sales, Carr remained essentially a loner. When the Canadian Group of Painters was formed in 1932, absorbing the Group of Seven and their ideology, she became one of the original members, but for her this and other art associations were simply exhibiting outlets.

At this time there was no adequate dealer system for contemporary Canadian art, and consequently the art societies had an important part to play. Artists banded together for mutual encouragement and support, to create opportunities for exhibition and discussion, to confer status, and to establish an awareness of and a voice for artists in a society that paid them little attention. Many artists felt both a responsibility and an exhilaration in taking part in the socializing aspects of these organizations which gave representation to their profession, but Carr was not a joiner in that sense; perhaps she was already too old for that kind of participation. Harris was the only major artist with whom she had a serious association based on a shared interest in art, and that was mostly by correspondence. In its early stages there was something of a master-acolyte relationship about it (as there was in her later friendship with Ira Dilworth). There seemed to be some deep-seated unease or distrust that prevented her from developing bonds with her peers. A.Y. Jackson, LeMoine Fitzgerald and J.W.G. (Jock) Macdonald were among those artists with whom she had friendly contacts that never developed into friendships.

Such activity and so much attention in this last and greatest period of her production must have given her satisfaction, but naturally there were intervals between exhibitions as well as periods when she had no reports on her work, and then she felt forgotten. In a bitter letter to Eric Brown in the fall of 1934, complaining that the National Gallery had yet to purchase something from her in the oil medium, she makes a somewhat self-pitying though revealing remark: "If the work of an isolated little old woman on the edge of nowhere is too *modern* for the Canadian National Gallery it seems to me it cannot be a very progressive institution."[1] And again, in April 1935, after an exhibition she had held in her flat: "How completely alone I've had to face the world, no boosters, no artist's backing, no relatives interested, no bother taken by papers to advertise, just me and an empty flat and the pictures. . . . How extraordinarily alone everyone is!"[2]

The occasional purchase of her work was encouraging, but sales were not sufficient to substantially affect Carr's economic situation until towards the close of the decade. In 1937, when she had her first heart attack and her financial needs became known, her friends rallied round and bought a number of paintings. In 1932 she had been offering full size oil-on-paper sketches to acquaintances for as little as ten or fifteen dollars. In the fall of 1938 she wrote to a friend that "money's a bit tight . . . unless I make an occasional sale I have *very* little to live on."[3] In another letter, this time to Ira Dilworth, probably in 1941 or 1942,[4] she wrote that her income was around $50 a month — $25 came from a small house she had traded her apartment for, she had a few bonds, and she received $15 monthly from a niece; out of that she paid Alice (the sister in whose house she was then living) $15 rent, and $20 to a maid.
There was still no strong support for art in Victoria, and many times a word of praise from distant parts must have seemed a little irrelevant. But Carr was no longer painting in isolation, and the Canadian art community was aware of her, and she of it. A second trip east in the spring of 1930 included a stay in New York during which she visited galleries, met Katherine Dreier and Georgia O'Keeffe, saw the work of Kandinsky, Braque, Duchamp (she mentions his "Nude Descending the Stairs"), Arthur Dove, Archipenko, Picasso and others. That and a 1933 trip to Chicago, even though the World's Fair art exhibition, which she had gone to see, had already closed when she arrived, must have contributed to a feeling of being part of a larger stream.

108   Within this period of travel and widening contacts around 1932, Carr, who already was

painting with impressive authority, began to show in her work a freedom and a quality of self-liberation. It took on expansiveness and flow; movement and rhythm replaced mass and weight; crowded interiors gave way to air and space. Compared to the heavily designed paintings of 1928-31, her later work appears to be less the product of the controlling mind and more that of the liberated spirit.

DEVELOPMENTS IN TECHNIQUE   Watercolour, along with drawing, was used as a note-taking and sketching medium throughout the earlier part of Carr's career, in fact until 1930. The practice, in common use by the Group of Seven and other contemporary artists, of sketching out-of-doors, using the oil medium on small, light wood panels that fitted into the lid of a sketch-box, was never adopted by her, though she did do a few exceptional sketches on wood panels.

Watercolour is not an easy medium to handle outdoors, especially in the difficult conditions Carr encountered on her northern trip to the Nass and Skeena river areas and to the Queen Charlotte Islands in the summer of 1928. Also, it did not relate to the formal problems she was starting to work on, problems of finding simplified form equivalents for the complexity of her subject material — trees, branches, the tangle of forest growth — which at that time in her expressive evolution she construed in terms of density, solidity and definition. Watercolour, because of its transparency and thinness, was not well suited to help her in that search, though she did a number of remarkable watercolours in which she overcame the shortcomings of the medium, often with the help of considerable underdrawing to strengthen the sense of mass and structure. The last dated watercolours are from her 1929 trip to Friendly Cove, though *Koskimo* appears to have been done in 1930. The problem remained of finding a sketching medium appropriate to her changing demands.

CHARCOAL DRAWINGS   Carr developed early the habit of drawing in any graphic medium as a means of recording, thinking or expressing. From her younger days there remains a range of delightful sketches of domestic incidents, as well as lighthearted pictorial comments on her travels in which she is often the centre of her own amusement. On her return from England in 1905 she did a series of cartoons for the Victoria newspaper *The Week*. She produced a prolific number of working drawings. In pencil, charcoal or brush these range from minor notes and fragments exploring a detail on a pole, the movement of a tree, a form relationship, to more developed compositions. The Newcombe Collection in Victoria contains dozens of such drawings, indicating the accumulation of observation and study that lies behind the completed works.

Around 1930-31, at the time she was moving away from her preoccupation with Indian themes, Carr did a number of large charcoal drawings on manila paper. A few are straightforward scenes, but most are conceptual studies in form, synthesizing experience and exploring ways of handling complex material. They are studio drawings, worked from less formulated material, and in their careful composition and quality of finish they form a coherent group — the refined product of a period of study, which she seems not to have repeated at any other time in her life. Several drawings explore the profound relationship she had discovered between the natural environment and the Indian's carvings. In these, carved eyes or eye-like shapes appear between dense, overlapping slab- and totem-like sections of foliage, for Carr perceived both the Indian's and nature's forms as having a common existence. Other drawings deal with trees and tree foliage or with clearings in the woods. Together they represent her search for formal equivalents for nature as she understood it, not its detail but its life, mystery and symbolic structure. These are her prototypes: the drape-like curtain of hanging foliage,

the swirling spiral of a young evergreen, the naked tree bole, the writhing stump, the living wall of jungle, and the vortex into the woods. Like the oils she did at this time, they assert an abstract pictorial space that replaces natural space. These charcoal drawings may have served as formal investigations for her paintings, but their worked-through completeness suggests that she also intended them for the independent works they are, even though they are neither signed nor dated and, with a few exceptions, are untitled and unidentified as to location.

OIL-ON-PAPER SKETCHES   "Sketching in the big woods is wonderful. You go, find a space wide enough to sit in and clear enough so that the undergrowth is not drowning you. Then, being elderly, you spread your camp stool and sit and look around. 'Don't see much here.' 'Wait.' Out comes a cigarette. The mosquitoes back away from the smoke. Everything is green. Everything is waiting and still. Slowly things begin to move, to slip into their places. Groups and masses and lines tie themselves together. Colours you had not noticed come out, timidly or boldly. In and out, in and out your eye passes. Nothing is crowded; there is living space for all. Air moves between each leaf. Sunlight plays and dances. Nothing is still now. Life is sweeping through the spaces. Everything is alive. The air is alive. The silence is full of sound. The green is full of colour. Light and dark chase each other. Here is a picture, a complete thought, and there another and there. . . . There are themes everywhere, something sublime, something ridiculous, or joyous, or calm, or mysterious. Tender youthfulness laughing at gnarled oldness. Moss and ferns, and leaves and twigs, light and air, depth and colour chattering, . . . you must be still in order to hear and see."[5]

When Carr turned away from the Indian theme, she no longer had to go far afield to find her material. Within a few miles of Victoria she could find endless variations on themes of sea and beach, light woods and deep forest, jungle and clearing — enough material to provide her with subjects for the rest of her painting life. Although in Victoria's mild climate there were locations available almost year round for a fine day's sketching, she liked to get outside the city where she could live close to nature for longer stretches of time. So developed her pattern of sketching trips, usually one in the spring and another in early autumn, with long intervals between for painting from the sketches in her studio and impatiently anticipating the next escape to nature. "What I am after is out there in the woods — even sketches to me are canned food. I like it fresh. Carry it right home and use it."[6]

Watercolour was no longer adequate for her changing expressive needs, and she had to find an alternative medium. Conventional artists materials were too expensive, especially because she liked to experiment freely, using "gallons of paint." Her search for an appropriate medium is indicated in a number of oil sketches on board, card or paper. Some are in monochromatic grey, black and white. In others, full colour is used for the exploration of tree and wooded interiors. Their pigment is thick in places and dry in texture, as the oil sank into the absorbent surface. Apparently they did not give her the fluidity she was looking for. There are also a number of free brush drawings of trees in black paint on paper. All these, and a group of oil-on-paper sketches — their very graphic character suggest they should be called drawings — done at Cordova Bay in the spring of 1931, might be regarded as developing models for the oil-on-paper paintings that constitute such an important part of her work from 1932 on.

The technique she developed for this medium was the essence of simplicity and practicality.[7] She bought quantities of cheap manila paper in large standard-size sheets and ordinary white house paint to mix with her artists colours. By using a lot of thinner (gasoline) with the pigment, she had a quick-drying medium with almost the fluidity of watercolour but with greater covering and structuring capacity. She described the

112

88

89

90

113

new medium in a letter to Eric Brown, who had mistaken one of the sketches for a watercolour: "It is a kind of sketchy medium I have used for the last three or four years. Oil paint used thin with gasoline on paper. . . . It is inexpensive, light to carry and allows great freedom of thought and action. Woods and skies out west are big. You can't squeeze them down."[8] Always ingenious, she devised a folding drawing board which would make the sketching equipment easier to handle.

Again in 1934, though still looking for the ultimate sketching material, she comments on how much she had learned from the paper-oils: "Freedom and *direction*. You are so unafraid to slash away because material scarcely counts. You use just can paint and there's no loss with failures. I try to do one almost every day. I make a sketch in the evening and a large paper sketch the following morning — or vice versa."[9] Sometimes she divided the sheet in halves, sometimes in quarters, and she mentions one day in which she got six paintings from one sheet.

After a day spent painting out-of-doors, back in camp at night she might work on the sketch again. There are canvases that relate to one, or perhaps several sketches, but the sketches vastly outnumber the canvases; they constitute a substantial and important part of her total work and have qualities quite their own. Inevitably, because oil-on-paper was a medium in which she could work freely, a greater proportion of weak paintings appear in this medium. In some early examples the considered design quality of coincident canvases continues to a degree, and the paper is often fairly consistently covered. Before long she was exploiting the full potential of the medium for obtaining sweep and movement, and she began to demonstrate the characteristics often seen in an artist's late work — spontaneous brushwork and a great deal of untouched ground.

Although Carr produced some of her most brilliant paintings in this inexpensive medium, there were problems with it. We know that one particularly concerned her: "Worked on some sketches that needed strengthening in expression. *The paper will not take enough studied labour*. If only one could combine spontaneity with more careful depth got through study."[10] A further concern has been the fragility of the sketches, for manila paper is very brittle and soon cracks and deteriorates unless mounted on a permanent and inert surface. Carr prepared them for exhibition in the early days by mounting them on mosquito netting, then fastening them at top and bottom to strips of wood. Late in 1938 she adopted the practice of gluing the paper to plywood, and the bonding agent in the plywood has had a deleterious effect on the paper.

From an artistic point of view the yellowing of the paper as it ages presents an additional problem. The sketches that were thinly painted and had large areas of untouched paper have altered considerably from their original colour and tone balance. The silver-white tonality has become yellow-brown and in some cases a light-dark tonal relationship has been reversed or equalized by time. Under varnish, which some collectors have applied, the paper turns a deep brown-orange. Because Carr used this technique essentially as a drawing medium in paint, the yellowing effects are less crucial than they might have been, and sometimes the resulting golden glow actually acts as a unifying element in the picture.

In the summer of 1933 Carr purchased a six-by-ten-foot van in which she, her pets and her equipment could be hauled to locations near Victoria, enabling her to live and work close to nature. She went by herself but was often visited by friends from town and by camp neighbours. Although her view of nature and her art precluded the presence of people in her paintings and permitted few tokens of their existence — fences, barns, shacks — she really liked to have people "not too near and not too far."[11] Between trips to the country, she could walk to her beloved Beacon Hill with

Untitled
oil on paper 91

BRITISH COLUMBIA FOREST
oil on paper 92

its cliffs, beach, sea and view across the strait, where she sketched on fine days throughout the year.

Her severe heart attack in January 1937 marked the beginning of increasingly failing health and a break in the regularity of the sketching sessions. The van was sold in the summer of 1938 after lying idle the previous year, and for subsequent trips Carr rented a cabin or house and hired a girl to do the housework. The last outing took place in 1942.

The contentment and joy she found in simple camp life (so vividly evoked in the Journals), especially during the several years she used the van, are typified by the freedom and directness she expressed in the sketches. "When I am tucked up there [her bed] I am very content, books on the shelf above my head and the good old coal-oil lamp. My sketches are under the bed, that other pile of thoughts, some good, some poor. When I lie cosy and the wind is howling round outside . . . I can peep out the little window beside the bed and feel for all the world like a chick peeping out of the feathers of an old Plymouth Rock. And there's all the lifey smells coming in and out through the flaps — hay and pine boughs and camp fire and puppies and cake and coal-oil and turps and paint and toilet soap and wash soap and powder and disinfectant and the rubber of the hot water bottle and mosquito oil. . . . but the camp fire and the hay and the pine trees are the strongest and compound them all into one sweetness. And the sounds of the trees and the birds that seem so much a part that you can't quite make out if they are in your own head or in the world."[12]

B.C. FOREST
oil on paper 94

ABSTRACT TREE FORMS
oil on paper 95

FOREST INTERIOR
oil on paper 96

94

95

118

A NEW LIBERATION

"A PICTURE EQUALS A MOVEMENT IN SPACE"   There was no break in activity or abrupt change in style, but the difference between Carr's work of, say, 1935 and that of her formal period is almost as radical as that between her formal and her French painting.

Having explored the dark, forbidding side of nature, Carr began to express its animating life and joy. She extended her range of nature themes to include, in addition to deep forest and jungle, more open woods, fields, airy tree-tops, beaches with open sky, and she made corresponding stylistic and expressive changes. When Carr had first seen Harris's work in 1927, she had been struck by his open, infinite, clear spaces, among which her "spirit seem[ed] able to leave [her] body and roam"[1]; they seemed to speak of the oneness of art and religion, and she wanted that oneness for herself. To achieve this goal, she made not space but movement her symbol for the expression of the "bigger something." Movement became her equation for life-force, for growth, for spiritual energy, for the struggle that is the condition of all life, for the consciousness of being part of a larger universe to which her writing refers and her painting aspires.

During 1934 and 1935 Carr's Journals make several allusions to her deliberately designed work of a few years earlier which she now finds to be limited. It is evident that she is in the process of clearing her thoughts for her emerging new phase of creation.

"A picture equals a movement in space. Pictures have swerved too much towards design and decoration. . . . The idea must run through the whole, the story that arrested you and urged the desire to express it, the story that God told you through that combination of growth. The picture side of the thing is the relationship of the objects to each other in one concerted movement, so that the whole gets up and goes, lifting the looker with it, sky, sea, trees affecting each other. Lines at right angles hold the eye fixed. Great care should be taken in the articulation of one movement into another so that the eye swings through the whole canvas with a continuous movement and does not find jerky stops, though it may be bucked occasionally with quick little turns to accelerate the motion of certain places. One must ascertain first whether your subject is a slow lolling one, or smooth flowing and serene, or quick and jerky, or heavy and ponderous."[2]

Having identified her central idea as movement, Carr proceeds to find movement in nature and to use it in her painting in different configurations. She uses it as a massive force: tilting cliffs; lifting sea into one rolling rhythm; bending the horizon into an arc; pushing forests to sea edge; creating an avalanche of undergrowth. *Shoreline* and *Rushing Sea of Undergrowth* are two canvases in which she has activated the forms of nature and endowed the rhythms of the painting with such a concept.

Ever since her contact with Harris, Carr had made use of light as an expressive element in her painting, but now she adds movement so that she can animate light to convey the expression of glory which she found in the sky. In a few paintings, such as *Scorned as Timber, Beloved of the Sky* with its whirling firmament, she comes close to an expression of ecstasy, a pure state of joyous identification with all nature.

At this time another variant in Carr's concept of movement or energy appears — a kind of atmospheric shimmer. A group of works illustrating this variant deals with her recurrent theme of tufted-topped, spindly trees. Among them are *Odds and Ends*, *Near Langford* and the related untitled sketch. In *Scorned as Timber, Beloved of the Sky*, with its radiance of centred, feathered light, or *Overhead* and *Above the Gravel Pits*, with their grand sweep of space, she is working from a concept of energy that belongs to the elements in nature themselves: the power of wind, the intensity of sun, the thrust of growth, and so on. In this new group, the forms of nature are still, so to speak; it is the atmosphere that vibrates. Here she conceives an energy that courses

through the air like a low-voltage electric charge, leaving the clumps of trees and the sky — everything — in a state of trembling motion. An early hint of this particular form of energy is seen in the molten, greyed, distant clump of trees profiled on the right-hand hill slope in *Above the Gravel Pit*. But in *Above the Trees* this particular energy is the essence of the painting, the upward-thrusting stumps retaining just enough of their own objective character to act as effective foil to the horizontal vibration which has affected sky, tree mass and earth and which dominates the universe.

Some of these works have a curious tropical feeling, partly the result of the vibrating, expansive atmosphere and the frequent pool of light in the middle distance, and partly because in a number of paintings tree trunks are painted in coarse horizontal patches of colour (as if to minimize their vertical structure) that suggest palm trees. In these paintings Carr comes close to an expressionist attitude in her work, for the psychic content of such movement hints at a mystic energy in the universe perceived by the nervous system rather than the eye.

As a consequence of Carr's concern with movement, all aspects of her picture-making gradually changed. In 1928 and 1929 paintings, she had visualized her trees, poles rocks and foliage as smoothly modelled, tangible, sculpted forms: solid and heavy. A group of her later paintings could be arranged, not necessarily in chronological order, to demonstrate a progression in which the solid matter of trees and rocks becomes, through the agency of such movement, more plastic and then deliquescent, finally vapourizing into air, light and space. Such a group might be: *A Young Tree*; *Deep Forest*; *Study in Movement*; *Above the Gravel Pit*; *Scorned as Timber, Beloved of the Sky*, and *Overhead*. In the last painting, the picture becomes virtually all sky as, like other artists who reached for transcendence, she attempts to convey infinite space.

The innovation of the oil-on-paper sketch played a large part in the development of Carr's concept of movement, since it allowed the brush to be used spontaneously, continuing large arm movements. The strokes thus become forms of movement in themselves, carrying expressive value as "smooth flowing and serene, or quick and jerky, or heavy and ponderous." The character of the sketches as drawing is often strong; in fact, many could be considered large coloured drawings. A late group is characterized by an energetic calligraphy that appears to have departed from nature to live a quivering, abstract life of its own. The movement of the brush may echo the modelling of a conical tree, or the shape of a cloud, but its primary value is movement, and to this end everything else is secondary: colour, flat or three-dimensional form, and tone. A few very late paintings are exceptions to this primacy of movement.

Carr's brush stroke becomes a carrier of expressive value and, at the same time, the unit of structure. It leaves its charge of pigment and the trace of its motion directly on the picture surface rather than blending them into an illusion of volumetric forms in space, as she had done before. Thus in this period she restores to her painting some of the visual immediacy of her French paintings. Of course the difference is that this immediacy no longer belongs to the optical effects of vibrant colour and textured pigment but results from Carr's concern for rhythm and movement.

A significant advance in her concept of space also occurs. At an early date she had adopted the convention of composing pictorial space in terms of foreground, middle ground and distance, a system implying that the viewer's space continues into that of the picture. Her adherence to this convention is often obvious throughout her work, especially her practice of creating an immediate foreground which might be a horizontal arrangement of rocks, rolling hillocks, stumps or logs. Sometimes these foregrounds appear contrived as though her imagination had failed her and she had filled them in out of habit and in obedience to convention. Increasingly in later works, now that her

124

Sketch relating to *A Rushing Sea of Undergrowth*
oil on paper 99

A RUSHING SEA OF UNDERGROWTH
oil on canvas 100

The last sketch of my van season is a study of underbrush and not successful. There is a sea of sallal and bracken, waving, surging, rolling towards you. Green jungle, thick yet loose-packed, solid, yet the very solidity full of air spaces. Perfectly ordered disorder designed with a helter-skelter magnificence. How can one express all this? To achieve it you must perch on a desperately uncomfortable log and dip among the roots for your material. Yet in spite of all the awkwardness there is a worthwhileness far exceeding a pretty sketch done at ease. There is a robust grandeur, loud-voiced, springing richly from earth untilled, unpampered, bursting forth rude, natural, without apology; an awful force greater in its stillness

than the crashing, pounding sea, more akin to our own elements than water, defying man, offering to combat with him, pitting strength for strength, not racing like the sea to engulf, to drown you but inviting you to meet it, waiting for your advance, holding out gently swaying arms of invitation. And people curse this great force, curse it for a useless litter because it yields no income. Run fire through this green sea, burn it, break it, make it black and frightful, tear out its roots! Leave it unguarded, forsaken, and from the bowels of the earth rushes again the great green ocean of growth. The air calls to it. The light calls to it. The moisture. It hears them. It is there waiting. Up it bursts; it will not be kept back. It is life itself, strong, bursting life.

Hundreds and Thousands, pp. 199-200

image is firmly anchored to the painting surface, she is able to put aside these arbitrary divisions and permit the picture to establish its own spatial system independent of the viewer. Paintings like *Sombreness Sunlit* or the sketches *Above the Trees* and *Untitled* (no. 109) demonstrate this new compositional freedom.

THE CHALLENGE OF MOUNTAINS   In mid-May of 1933 Carr left home for a working expedition into the high mountain country north of Vancouver, going by rail to Brackendale and Pemberton, past Anderson and Seton lakes, and on to Lillooet. On the return she stopped at the Durban House at Seton. On 7 June she writes of "mountains towering — snow mountains, blue mountains, green mountains, brown mountains, tree-covered, barren rock, cruel mountains with awful waterfalls and chasms and avalanches, tender mountains all shining, spiritual peaks way up among the clouds."[3] The mountain, which is earth-based yet aspires to infinity, was a preoccupying theme for Harris at that time and reflected his theosophic belief. Carr's association with Harris was still very close, and doubtless his preoccupation stimulated her pursuit. Her mountain paintings, however, had nothing to do with the austere spirituality of Harris's Arctic-inspired works. By 1933 her art was becoming increasingly spontaneous in its reflection of her experience and concern with movement.

In several paintings done either on or as a result of this trip, Carr tackles the problem of painting the mountain at close range where she has to deal with its bulk and immobility and brooding presence — qualities more in sympathy with her mood of a year or two earlier. She records in the Journals her painful struggle with *The Mountain*,[4] which lasted nearly three months: it "might be a cardboard stage set, not an honest dirt-and-rock solidity of immovableness"[5]; but she did succeed in capturing the "great dominating strength and spirit brooding there,"[6] while investing its folds and hollows with the surging movement she had begun to equate with life-force. But more often, in paintings like *Lillooet Indian Village* or *Village in the Hills*, she pushes the mountains into the distance so that she can exploit their silhouettes or contours in the interest of large rolling rhythms in space, rather than having to contend with their pressing mass. Despite a number of works dealing successfully with the subject, the mountain was not to become a continuing source of inspiration for her, as it was for Harris. The mountains of the Olympic Peninsula or of Vancouver Island continued to appear in the distance in Carr's paintings of beach or cliff with sea and sky, but never again did she make them the focus of attention in her work.

102

103

104

THE MOUNTAIN
oil on canvas 106

HOUSES BELOW THE
MOUNTAIN
oil on paper 107

SOMBRENESS SUNLIT
oil on canvas 108

106

107

Untitled
oil on paper 109

ODDS AND ENDS
oil on canvas 110

ABOVE THE GRAVEL PIT
oil on canvas 111

I started a new canvas today, a skyscape with roots and gravel pits.
I am striving for a wide, open sky with lots of movement, which is
taken down into dried greens in the foreground and connected by
roots and stumps to sky. My desire is to have it free and jubilant,
not crucified into one spot, static. The colour of the brilliantly lighted
sky will contrast with the black, white and tawny earth.

Hundreds and Thousands, p. 293

OVERHEAD
oil on paper 112

LILLOOET INDIAN VILLAGE
oil on canvas 113

ROCKS BY THE SEA
oil on paper 114

Upon my screen are pinned two sketches; one is of a great stump
in a sea of whirly green . . . the other is a great mounded cliff of
clay covered with shaggy dried cliff grass — it is weighted and heavy,
it ends abruptly on the end of the paper, no beach or anything
below. There is a heavy blue sky, broken and tucked behind; the
mound has that heavy cumbersomeness like the hindquarters of
a bear.

from an undated letter to Ira Dilworth 1942 or 1943, Public Archives of Canada

A NEW INTEGRATION

PAINTING, THE TOTALITY OF EXPERIENCE   The convention equating
seriousness and importance in art with permanence, and therefore, in the case of
painting, favouring oil-on-canvas over other media, still prevailed in the thirties, and
at first Carr did not attach much value to her work in oil-on-paper. However, well
before the autumn of 1935 when she held an exhibition of sketches in Toronto — an
exhibition to which Graham McInnes gave high praise in *Saturday Night* — they had
become an important part of her output, permitting a whole range of expression, from
tentative or fragmentary ideas to more comprehensive statements. (The word "sketch"
is a convenient term which we still use but which does not always suggest the significance of individual works.)

The fact is that Carr's paper paintings not only mark the emergence of the liberated
Carr but also herald a consistency that operates at all levels of her art. In creating the
large body of sketches to add to her oeuvre, Carr permits us to witness both the creative
impulse at its freshest and the considered statement, without having to shift the focus
of our vision. The great conceptual canvases of her formal period, such as *Nirvana,
Old Time Coast Village* or *Potlatch Welcome*, were based on drawings or watercolours
very different from the resulting canvases. Measured in terms of the transforming act
of the imagination and the deliberate formal reshaping that took place, the distance
separating the drawing or watercolour and the canvas in those works is considerable.
In her later years, however, the paper sketch and the canvas employ essentially the
same vision and have the same expressive intention. The canvases in the main represent
just a transfer to another medium that calls for a greater degree of completion, and the
chief problem they pose for Carr is how she can retain the fervour and immediacy of
her sketches.

The proliferating papers and the canvases flow on the same level in the imagination
and ask to be seen together — taken in great gulps as well as viewed individually —
so that the accumulative effect of a generic idea that has multiplied into a number of
variations can be felt. Carr wrote to Ira Dilworth, probably in 1941 or 1942, "Today
I have worked hard on a mysterious little bit, little round umbrella trees, spindly runts
who grew up under forest giants that have been reduced to timber long since."[1] We do
not know which particular little round umbrella trees Carr was working on when she
wrote that letter, but we do know that the idea was alive in her imagination over a long
time, for it appeared as early as 1935 in *Loggers' Culls* and *Scorned as Timber, Beloved
of the Sky*. It is interesting to see together the latter canvas and the three paper sketches,
all of which deal with that theme. Clearly the sketch without the left-hand clump of
trees is the one that relates most directly to the canvas, though the thematic idea is
common to all three. The other two sketches similarly belong together, but *Edge of the
Forest* is closer to a canvas, being more finished in its painting and more developed
conceptually. The foreground is worked out to include stumps which emphasize the
dramatic point; the height of the tree and its spindliness are emphasized. Other changes
can be noted: the striated, flame-like sky rather than whirling discs; the rippling,
horizontal, ribbon-like striations that meld the clump of trees together, all of which
suggest that this is a slightly later sketch developed from the first.

The perceptual consistency between her sketches and canvases is progressive, and in
certain late canvases, like *Sombreness Sunlit* and *Dancing Sunlight*, the gap between
these two phases of an artist's work — phases which so often represent different creative
intentions — almost disappears.

The fluidity of the oil-on-paper technique permitted Carr to give form to an idea almost
at the speed of thought so that inspiration, always elusive, had less inclination to falter
in an encounter with resistant, heavy pigment. This is one reason why the paper
sketches were so important in the late stages of her evolution, for in her mature creative
process, form follows feeling, a sequence that places a great burden on inspiration.

But despite the great strengths that this approach to painting revealed in Carr, it allowed her moments of weakness. During the preceding formal period in her work, the creative process was more drawn out. Those earlier paintings were based on an architectonic structure that could be carefully worked out in advance, and altered and corrected a step at a time in the actual execution of the canvas. The tension, essential to any successful work, in those paintings is a matter of the articulation of form; this she could control and elaborate on at any stage. But in the later work, when movement, spontaneity and gesture replaced formal structure as her primary mode, the necessary tension had to be found elsewhere: in the quality of line itself, or in the rhythms. This is when the occasional failure in inspiration allows the painting gesture to flag, revealing itself in forms that have lost their elasticity or wiriness. We find this occurring most often when she is dealing with large-scale rhythms, or when her vision becomes self-consciously exalted.

An attempt might be made to classify Carr's abundant output during these years, chronologically or by subject matter — deep forest, clearings, sea and sky, and so on — but both these systems seem to be incidental and even irrelevant, for her art is at this time completely integrated with the totality of her experience. Perhaps her paintings are best seen as expressions of certain primary experiences which to some degree she projected on nature, and of course the reverse — discovered through nature. Some of these experiences had begun to assert themselves in her art long before, as in the dim woodland interiors of Stanley Park of 1909-10 — but in the 1930s her paintings became free of all reference except to nature itself, which had now become her central and all-sufficient theme: nature as life-force.

Looked at this way, Carr's paintings fall into natural groups centring around a number of primary elements: space, inviting or expansive, or, in its absence, crowding; light, glowing or radiant, or its mysterious counterpart, dark; movement and its compulsive sweep or its nervous tremble; mass whose inert strength resists animation. Sometimes the central experience is one of ecstasy — the experience of identity with all creation. These are the large "ideas" or "essences" Carr sought when she went out into nature with her sketching equipment, and she found manifestations of them over and over again — in sea and sky; in the hollow at the heart of the forest; in the claustrophobic jungle; in light penetrating the forest darkness; in the infinity of sky. Such themes abounded in the nature that she studied, and she explored and absorbed them endlessly. They also corresponded to deep emotional states within herself, and she had her own well-developed form concepts and a continually expanding pictorial vocabulary for expressing them. Carr is not the only artist to have achieved the necessary integration between observed outer reality and inner self, together with those pictorial skills that relate hand and eye, but she is distinguished by the elemental level at which the integration takes place, so that she is wholly and inseparably present in everything she creates.

All the underlying content in Carr's painting becomes modified within her free and expansive mood. For instance, there is much sublimated eros in her work, and some imagery of strong sexual connotation was frequent in the formal painting period: the contained hollows and openings in the woods; the phallic poles, stumps and tree trunks. Such content does not disappear in her later work but is translated into a powerful and more generalized sexual energy, as openings and enclosures vibrate with light and movement, trunks thrust upward into sky, earth fecundates, and death and decay are absorbed into the irresistible regenerative cycle. The expression of such primary content was inevitable in her work once she had succeeded in painting out of her deepest self, and when she found in nature her comprehensive metaphor for life, one that provided her with images capable of dealing with the whole of her experience. It is part of her great achievement that she created a mature form that

Sketch relating to *Scorned as Timber, Beloved of the Sky*
oil on paper 116

THE PINE TREE
oil on paper 117

was capable of carrying this sexual content and giving it statement of archetypal force.

To anyone familiar with Carr's writing, her tendency to animate every thing with life is a prominent characteristic. Whether it has the effect of marvellously sharpening the prose, as it often does, or of cloying it, as it sometimes does, the habit is ingrained. As she becomes familiar with her van it ceases to be the "elephant" and becomes the "motherly old hen"[2]; the mountains which resist her as she tries to paint them will not "brood like great sitting hens,"[3] and one is like a "great corsetless woman"[4]; the little pines wear "sticking-out petticoats"[5]; and so on. Her literary images are consistently and delightfully homey. All this is part of her infectious joy and participation in the sensory side of life — tastes, sounds, smells, sights — as well as her passion for animals. In camp one morning, thinking how sensible it would be to bathe by rolling naked in the sopping grass, she remarks: "The *liveness* in me just loves to feel the *liveness* in growing things, in grass and rain and leaves and flowers and sun and feathers and fur and earth and sand and moss. The touch of those is wonderful."[6]

The seeing of things in metaphor is partly the artist's way, but the empathizing nature of Carr's metaphor — her frequent anthropomorphizing — relates to her instinctive animism. She was of the earth — Mother Earth — and so it was natural for her to endow inanimate objects with human life, humans with animal life or vice versa, nature with spirit life, or any other combination. It was as though, through all the layers of training and conditioning, she had managed, like some educated primitive, to hang on to a vestige of primal spirit affinity with all the forms of creation. This view of the connectedness of things found reinforcement, clarification and added spiritual meaning in the attitudes of many others whom she encountered during her life: those of the Indian who in his art expressed his view of himself as part of all existence, natural and spiritual; those expressed by Walt Whitman in his poetry; and those she found in her own brand of non-doctrinaire Christianity.

The anthropomorphism in Carr's writing has its echo in her painting. In a number of paintings of the 1928-31 period she demonstrates a theatrical approach. For instance, in *Forest, British Columbia* she conceives the composition as a stage set, with hanging curtains of foliage admitting top lighting and tree trunks lined up to give access to the wings. As in the writing, nature forms are personified and assigned roles: the young, dancing, joyous tree performing on stage, surrounded by sober and sympathetic elders (*The Little Pine*); the young tree, green with bursting growth, older generations of trees behind and, completing the cycle, the dead uprooted log at the foot of the stage (*A Young Tree*). The heavens, as always, are part of the established mood in such paintings, with skies darkening or brightening, or, as in *Forsaken*, sending a falling shaft of light onto the lone mortuary box almost awash in the sea of undergrowth. Her pictorial form has responded to a theatrical or literary sentiment, and at times such meanings are quite explicit, but after 1932 they tend to be absorbed into a larger pantheism and into her unity of movement. In *Reforestation*, for instance, the "stage" has dissolved and the "actors" (young trees, middle-aged trees, etc.) submerge their roles into the "great, big, huge, enormous something supreme."[7] And in many other paintings, among them *Above the Gravel Pit* and *Shoreline*, everything is movement; sky, distant forest, horizon are caught in a common swell, and the brush becomes activator rather than narrator or shaper. In *Scorned as Timber, Beloved of the Sky* a radiance of central light animated by brush strokes of lambent colour is the main agent of expression, and there is little to remind us of specific emotive content apart from that self-conscious title chosen to identify it in exhibition. In *Overhead* even that reminder is gone, as a trembling luminosity irradiates the picture space and becomes the expressive property of the work as a whole. Here too, as in other sea-sky paintings, the arch of the sky draws the horizon into an answering bow, a late continuation of the ovoid motif used in much of her earlier work.

143

Carr, during this time of maturity, gives continued though altered expression to nature's darker side. *Strangled by Growth* was an early expression of inimical nature for which the totem poles and their equally brooding settings had provided a vehicle — for a while to the exclusion of all else. The eye form, so prominent in the Indian's art, with its expressive value as watching, silent presence, Carr often echoed in her forest forms as openings between foliage and branches. In the canvas *Zunoqua of the Cat Village* (Carr tells the story behind this painting in *Klee Wyck*) the cats, another form of nature, swimming and drowning in the engulfing sea of green share the communication of the demonic spirit with the forest and the carving. The eyes in the forest behind are both the cats' eyes and the spirit eyes of the place. That this is a transitional canvas, painted in 1931 when the Indian theme was still lingering, even though she had already made up her mind to move into nature, is supported by the relatively fluid concept of the growth as compared to 1928-29 paintings. In *Roots*, painted four or five years later, the literal reference is gone. Her intuitive response to dank jungle and her perception of the demonic possibilities of the rearing stump and up-turned root allow her to enter directly into their life without overt reference or superfluous drama. If she is aware of the "eye" in the monster root, she gives no hint, allowing the looker to find it for himself.

A MEASURE OF ABSTRACTION   The frequent aspect of the Journals as invocation to spiritual powers should not obscure their revelation of Carr the constant artist, thinking about form, pondering the means of translating her experience into painting terms. The form-complex she developed in such paintings as *White Church*, with its cubist-derived elements, and with the help of Harris and Tobey, was a kind of layering of three-dimensional, stylized forms. They show what a superb designer she was. Her form language at this stage (1928-29) is considerably abstract, but it points to a sculptural concept of abstraction rather than a pictorial one. Like other aspects of her work, this too underwent change.

When Harris, after the mid-1930s, turned in his own work to abstraction, Carr found his work beautiful and deeply moving, and his ideas on the subject tremendously interesting, even though she could not accept them herself. But did she realize how closely her practice paralleled his advice to her: "When, in your letter, you refer to 'movement in space,' that is abstract, try it. . . . Take an idea, abstract its essence. Rather, get the essence from Nature herself, give it new form and intensity. You have the 'innards' of the experience of nature to go by and have done things which are so close to abstraction that you should move into the adventure much more easily than you perhaps think."[8] Did she realize, in her pursuit of essence and in her mystical involvement with nature, just how abstract in quality some of her work of the late thirties had become?

Swaying and an untitled forest interior carry over what she had learned from her earlier design studies in formal composing and patterning; in addition the imagery in those paintings has moved considerably away from their starting place in nature. The long sweeps of pigment, the gestural hatchings and ripples that relate to trees and growth, the tone reversals and sensitivity to positive and negative space which characterizes the handling of stump areas — the total energy of the paintings' surfaces — demand an abstract reading. Of course their origin in nature remains clear, but a new and powerful tension results from the degree and kind of abstraction in their statement. Whether or not they were painted in 1937 is unclear, but they relate to a statement she made then about her tackling canvases "with huge brush strokes, first going for the movement and direction such as I got in my sketches, and with great freedom. The danger in canvases is that of binding and crucifying the emotion, of pinning it there to die flattened on the surface. Instead, one must let it move over

DANCING SUNLIGHT
oil on canvas 119

FOREST LIGHT
oil on canvas 120

144

the surface as the spirit of God moved over the face of the waters."9

The kind of abstraction towards which such canvases were pointing was quite different from her earlier work and naturally from that of Lawren Harris. Her route by this time was becoming expressionist, immediate, based in the senses though informed by spirit; his was remote, removed, metaphysical, rooted in contemplation and silence. In any case her most energetic painting years were over and that particular "adventure" was not to be pursued.

FOREST INTERIOR IN SHAFTS
OF LIGHT
oil on canvas 121

FOREST
oil on canvas 122

TREES, GOLDSTREAM FLATS
oil on canvas 123

BLUE SKY
oil on paper 124

122

123

WEST COAST FOREST
OF GREAT TREES
oil on paper 125

CORDOVA DRIFT
oil on canvas 126

WOOD INTERIOR
oil on canvas 127

125

126

150

RED CEDAR
oil on canvas 128

BOLE OF A TREE
oil on paper 129

Untitled
oil on paper 130

TREE
oil on paper 131

REFORESTATION
oil on canvas 132

YOUNG AND OLD FOREST, B.C.
(Sketch relating to *Something Unnamed*)
oil on paper 133

REBIRTH (original title *Something Unnamed*)
oil on canvas 134

132

154

There is nothing so strong as growing. Nothing can drown that force that splits rocks and pavements and spreads over the fields. . . . Man can pattern it and change its variety and shape, but leave it for even a short time and off it goes back to its own, swamping and swallowing man's puny intentions. No killing nor stamping down can destroy it. Life is in the soil. Touch it with air and light and it bursts forth like a struck match. Nothing is dead, not even a corpse. It moves into the elements when the spirit has left it, but even to the spirit's leaving there is life, boundless life, resistless and marvellous, fresh and clean, God.

Hundreds and Thousands, p. 301

133

134

Three new pictures are on the way, an immense wood, a wood edge and a woods movement. These woods movements should be stupendous, the inner burstings of growth showing through the skin of things, throbbing and throbbing to burst their way out. . . .

When you want depth in a woods picture avoid sharp edges and contrasts. Mould for depth, letting the spaces sink and sink back and back, warm alternating with cool colour. Build and build forward and back.

Hundreds and Thousands, pp. 295-96

135

YOUNG ARBUTUS
oil on paper 135

FOREST LANDSCAPE II
oil on paper 136

Untitled
oil on paper 137

LAUGHING FOREST
oil on paper 138

136

137

I am camping in Mrs. Shadforth's little one-room shack on Craig-flower Road. It is . . . set upon a ridge among unspoiled trees, tall firs, little pines, scrub, arbutus bushes and maples. . . .

The colours are brightening, rich and deep under the wet. The arbutus leaves are new and tender, not finished and done like the others. It has thrown off the old bark of its limbs in crinkly little rolls and under them the new bark is satin-smooth, orange and red and green-gold.

Hundreds and Thousands, September 1929, pp. 305-06

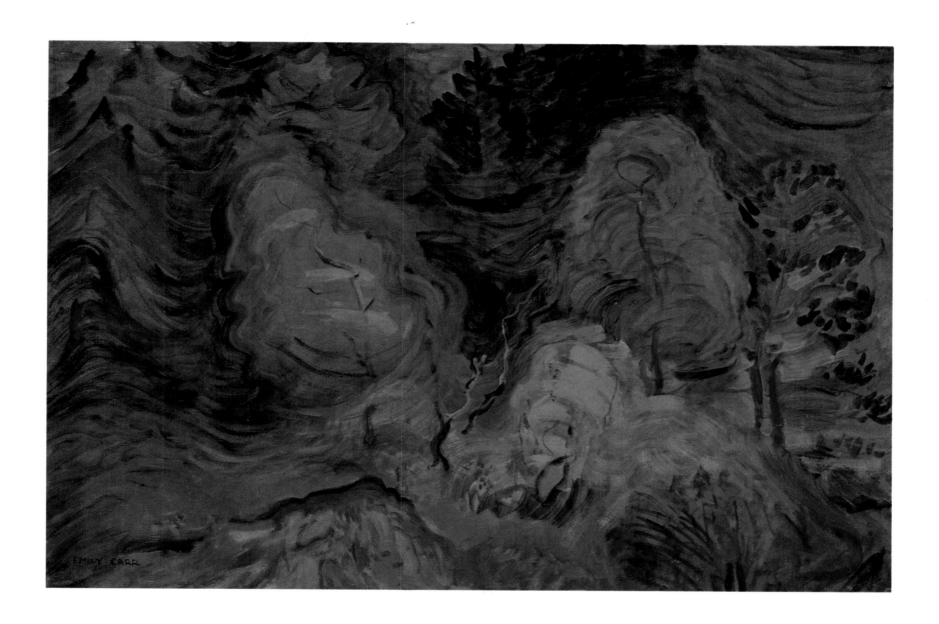

158

SWIRL
oil on canvas 139

YOUNG PINES AND SKY
oil on paper 140

B.C. TREES
oil on paper 141

140

141

The pliability of growth is marvellous. The limbs that have life in them bend and toss and sway but they do not break. Just the dead ones snap. Life springs back joyously. It's one continuous battle with the elements here, rain, wind or heat. Moderation is at a premium.

This is a place of high skies, blue and deep and seldom cloudless. I have been trying to express them and made a poor fist of it. Everything is eternally on the quiver with wind. It runs on the short dry grass and sluices it as if the earth were a jelly. The trees in shelter stand looking at the wobbly ones in the wind's path, like a strange pup watches two chum pups playing, a little enviously. I think trees love to toss and sway; they make such happy noises.

Hundreds and Thousands, p. 186

142

143

FOREST CLEARING
oil on paper 145

NEAR LANGFORD B.C.
oil on canvas 146

LOGGERS' CULLS
oil on canvas 147

STUMPS AND SKY
oil on paper 148

On days like today the relationship between the trees and the sky is very close. That, I think, is what makes a picture, a thought so expressed that the relationship of all the objects is shown to be in their right place. I used to paint a picture and stick in an interesting sky with clouds etc. that would decoratively balance my composition. It wasn't part of the conception of the whole. Now I know that the sky is just as important as the earth and the sea in working out the thought.

Hundreds and Thousands, p. 187

151

152

I am nearer sixty-nine than sixty-eight now, and a long way recovered
from my stroke [5 June]. . . . Maybe I shall go out into the woods
sketching again, who knows? I have got the sketches out that I did
on the trip just before my stroke. They are very full of spring joy,
high in key, with lots of light and tenderness of spring. How did
I do these joyous things when I was so torn up over the war?

Hundreds and Thousands, pp. 324-25

FIR TREE AND SKY
oil on canvas 155

SWAYING
oil on canvas 156

168

I am painting a sky. A big tree butts up into it on one side, and there is a slope in the corner with pines. These are only to give distance. The subject is sky, starting lavender beneath the trees and rising into a smoother hollow air space, greenish in tone, merging into laced clouds and then into deep, bottomless blue, not flat and smooth like the centre part of the sky, but loose, coming forward. There is to be one sweeping movement through the whole air, an ascending movement, high and fathomless. The movement must connect with each part, taking great care with the articulation. A movement floating up. It is a study in movement, designed movement — very subtle.

Hundreds and Thousands, p. 170

There's a torn and splintered ridge across the stumps I call the "screamers." These are the unsawn last bits, the cry of the tree's heart, wrenching and tearing apart just before she gives that sway and the dreadful groan of falling, that dreadful pause while her executioners step back with their saws and axes resting and watch. It's a horrible sight to see a tree felled, even now, though the stumps are grey and rotting. As you pass among them you see their screamers sticking up out of their own tombstones, as it were. They are their own tombstones and their own mourners.

Hundreds and Thousands, pp. 132-33

157

FOREST LANDSCAPE
oil on paper 157

FOREST
oil on canvas 158

Untitled
oil on canvas 159

Working on jungle. . . . nobody goes there. . . . The loneliness repels
them, the density, the unsafe hidden footing, the dank smells, the
great quiet, the mystery, the general mix-up (tangle, growth, what
may be hidden there), the insect life. They are repelled by the awful
solemnity of the age-old trees, with the wisdom of all their years
of growth looking down upon you, making you feel perfectly in
infinitesimal — their overpowering weight, their groanings and
creekings, mutterings and sighings — the rot and decay of the old
ones — the toadstools and slugs among the upturned, rotting roots
of those that have fallen, reminding one of the perishableness of
even those slow-maturing, much-enduring growths. . . . The sallal
is tough and stubborn, rose and blackberry thorny. There are the
fallen logs and mossy stumps, the thousand varieties of growth and
shapes and obstacles, the dips and hollows, hillocks and mounds,
riverbeds, forests of young pines and spruce piercing up through
the tangle to get to the quiet light diluted through the overhanging
branches of great overtopping trees. Should you sit down, the great,
dry, green sea would sweep over and engulf you.

Hundreds and Thousands, p. 207

SKY
oil on paper 162

SEASCAPE
oil on paper 163

STRAIT OF JUAN DE FUCA
oil on paper 164

Untitled
oil on paper 165

174

I woke up this morning with "unity of movement" in a picture strong in my mind. I believe Van Gogh had that idea. I did not realize he had striven for that till quite recently so I did not come by the idea through him. It seems to me that clears up a lot. I see it very strongly out on the beach and cliffs. I felt it in the woods but did not quite realize what I was feeling. Now it seems to me the first thing to seize on in your layout is the direction of your main movement, the sweep of the whole thing as a unit. One must be very careful about the transition of one curve of direction into the next, vary the length of the wave of space but *keep it going*, a pathway for the eye and the

mind to travel through and into the thought. For long I have been trying to get these movements of the parts. Now I see there is only *one* movement. It sways and ripples. It may be slow or fast but it is only one movement sweeping out into space but always keeping going — rocks, sea, sky, one continuous movement.

Hundreds and Thousands, pp. 106-07

LAST PERIOD

RETURN TO THE INDIAN THEME   Although the publishing of her books did not start until late in her life Carr had been working on her stories for many years. Clearly, writing was a compulsive form of expression for her, like painting, and she seemed able to swing from one to the other in some creative rhythm beneficial to both. "Pulled out my summer sketches and tried to get busy. It wouldn't come. I got to the typewriter and described Fort Rupert minutely, its looks and feeling and thoughts. Then I got to some charcoal drawing and commenced to *feel* it but got nothing very definite."[1]

After her first heart attack and lengthy convalescence in early 1937, her health was increasingly frail, and her energy for the more physically demanding painting was curtailed. More time was devoted to writing, and this activity had a particular effect on the painting: as her ability to seek fresh material and her stamina generally diminished, she began to draw more on earlier sketches and recollections. Working on the Indian stories during her convalescence obviously triggered her return to Indian paintings. In April 1937, barely out of hospital, she reported: "I have been painting all day, with four canvases on the go — Nass pole in undergrowth, Koskimo, Massett bear, and an exultant wood."[2] (*Massett Bears* was among four paintings sent off to Vancouver for exhibition that spring, and the well-known *Forsaken* is almost certainly the Nass pole in undergrowth.) Again, in May 1941, she wrote to a friend: "Going over Indian sketches [stories] has stirred up a homesickness for Indian."[3]

Some of Carr's stories were read on the radio in 1940, and the preparation for the publication of *Klee Wyck* included the idea of a coincident exhibition.[4] The exhibition did not materialize, but its possibility gave particular purpose and focus for her "homesickness." *Laughing Bear*, which appears on the cover of *Klee Wyck*'s paperback edition, was painted for her publisher in connection with the first edition, and other Indian paintings done in 1941 were stimulated by her interest in the book.

In July 1941 Carr wrote in a letter to Ruth Humphrey of "five new Indian ones nearly finished."[5] These probably included *A Skidegate Pole* and *Skidegate Beaver Pole*, which in their carefully finished execution are in contrast with other late Indian paintings where she uses a coarse brush in the loose and spontaneous manner of some of the woodscapes. They also offer interesting comparison with the 1912 canvases of the same subjects to which they clearly owe their origin. In her mood of relative calm she abandons the narrow vertical margins of the earlier paintings for a near-square format — unusual for her — permitting more lateral space; by this time the pole is seen less as the feature of interest and more as a participant in all creation. In *A Skidegate Pole*, a grey truncated pole takes on a pearly glow in the undulating and luminous radiance of sky and undifferentiated green growth. Like *Grey* of an earlier time, *A Skidegate Pole* is one of those paradigmatic works that bring together an accumulation of experience in one concentrated statement, marking the completion of a phase, freeing the artist for new ideas.

PORTRAITS   During the winter months of 1931-32 Carr had been working on portrait heads — "thinking it would get a little green out of my eye"[6] — with Edythe Hembroff, a close friend of the thirties, who, under the name Hembroff-Schleicher, is the author of two books on Carr. By March of 1938 Carr was, in her own words, "wrestling again with my forest. Trees are so much more sensible than people, steadier and more enduring."[7] None of these earlier heads seem to have survived, unless the little rear view painting of the back of her head on card in the Vancouver Art Gallery collection is one of them. At the end of 1938 she was once again working on portraits, "turning from my beloved woods for fear that all this honeyed stuff, this praise, should send me to them smug."[8] Fortunately, several of these portrait sketches have survived,

including two studies of her maid Shirley, one of which is on loan to the Art Gallery of Ontario. Among this late group is also the splendid self-portrait, executed with spontaneous and summary sureness; it has been well described by Ruth Humphrey, a close friend who helped Carr with her writing, as "rather severe, but very like Emily when disturbed and in her painting smock, glaring at an intruder through her specs."[9] It shows the plump and aging Carr, now in her late sixties and wearing the practical, loose, nondescript garment and little net cap over her hair so often seen in photographs of her.

On the last day of 1940 she was thinking once again about portraits. "I hate painting portraits. I am embarrassed at what seems to me to be an impertinence and presumption, pulling into visibility what every soul has as much right to keep private as his liver and kidneys and lungs and things. . . . The better a portrait, the more indecent and naked the sitter must feel. An artist who portrays flesh and clothes but nothing else, . . . is quite harmless. . . . To paint a self-portrait should teach one something about oneself. I shall try."[10] If she followed this advice to herself the results have not so far come to light.

LAST NATURE PAINTINGS   It is possible that *The Clearing*, a dated work of 1942 in the National Gallery's collection, was Carr's last oil painting, as Lawren Harris stated in his catalogue essay for the major Carr exhibition of 1945 shown at the Art Gallery of Toronto and the National Gallery in Ottawa. There are other paintings of that year, however. She was afraid that the sketches resulting from her 1942 trip to Mount Douglas Park would be rather sombre when seen in exhibition, but, she said, sombreness "is the character of the woods there-about . . . they [the woods] were *not* sad, it was a very happy session in my cabin there at Mount Douglas Park."[11] Their fault is not that they are sombre — much of her great work is that — but that they often reflect a diminished élan, usually a marked characteristic in her sketches, without compensating qualities.

In addition to *The Clearing*, two other canvases of 1942, *Cedar* and *Quiet*, represent her more favourably in her late work. They do not enlarge on her cumulative vision of nature but restate aspects of it in a mood of lyrical tranquillity. The uncomfortable sense of striving for identification with the forces underlying nature, which marked a few earlier works, is gone. One would like to think that this note of calm reflects a well-earned peace of mind now that her long life-journey through painting was nearly over.

For the previous five years Emily Carr had been living at 218 St. Andrews Street, Victoria, in the house of her remaining sister, Alice, which had been altered to provide Emily with her own living and working quarters. Alice's sight was almost gone and Emily's health had seriously deteriorated; they needed each other, and it was easier being under the same roof.

In 1943 and 1944 Carr was able to paint a little, and she even worked in the early months of 1945 on some of her old oil-on-paper sketches in preparation for an exhibition that was to have taken place in Vancouver in April. After completing the sketches, mounting them on plywood, framing them, preparing lists of them and arranging for their shipment, she felt suddenly tired. She packed up her typewriter and some paper and went to St. Mary's Priory, a Catholic nursing home, for a rest. There, less than a week later, on 2 March, she died after the last of many heart attacks she had suffered over the previous eight years. She did not live to receive the honorary doctorate which was to have been given her that spring by the University of British Columbia.

LAUGHING BEAR
oil on paper 170

MASSET BEARS
oil on canvas 171

A SKIDEGATE BEAVER POLE
oil on canvas 172

171

172

At Gittex there was a wooden bear on top of such a high pole that
he was able still to look over the top of the woods. He was a joke
of a bear — every bit of him was merry. He had one paw up against
his face, he bent forward and his feet clung to the pole. I tried to
circle about so that I could see his face but the monstrous tangle
was impossible to break through.

Klee Wyck, p. 53

QUIET
oil on canvas 175

CEDAR SANCTUARY
oil on paper 176

EMILY CARR

EPILOGUE

SELF-PORTRAIT
oil on paper 177

A CONTEXT OF "FRESH SEEING"   Carr's idealism and naiveté had kept her from understanding the ambivalent nature of the art world, or her own needs. She distrusted the art-educated and at one time worked hard to stir up enthusiasm and raise support for a People's Art Gallery[1] which would be housed in her House of All Sorts. She dreamed of painting "so simply that the common ordinary people would understand and see something of God in your expressing. The educated look for technique and pattern, colour quality, composition. Spirit touches them little and it's the only thing that counts."[2] She obviously had in mind a "hypothetical" ordinary people, not the "real" ordinary people who gauged her success in terms of prices and sales and who asked the literal questions that exasperated her.

But while Carr wanted acceptance by the ordinary community around her, she depended — although she resisted the thought — on the art-educated, whose approval could give her a professional reputation and ultimately a livelihood. Their lack of interest and erratic support on the one hand and their self-interested posturings on the other she found wanting and affected.

Popularity, reputation and critical acclaim do not always come together, but Carr has had a measure of all three since her death, and some even before. Her unpretentious and engaging writing became popular first, beginning with *Klee Wyck*, which was an almost immediate success upon publication in 1941. Many people do not know her painting at all; others have been led to it through her writing. Today large numbers are unfamiliar with her writing and her painting but know her by reputation as a woman of admirable eccentricity, a legend disseminated through television and radio programs and references in fiction and poetry which assume that she is part of the Canadian culture.

Carr's painting has more slowly, though surely, gained the Canadian audience it deserves, and recent shifts in social and cultural attitudes are serving to bring it into broader attention in a climate of "fresh seeing." Her interest in the Indian and her passion for a nature uncontaminated by man have attracted those who are sympathetic to the environmental and human rights movements. She embodied the Indians' art in her own, and her writing conveys respect for them as a people and fondness for those she knew. Carr's longstanding friendship with the Indian Sophie, which survived her painful discovery that the Indian woman was a drunkard and a prostitute, is frequently referred to by Carr and is the subject of one of her stories. Large cities, except for fleeting visits, literally sickened her, and only in nature did she feel whole. These themes of Indian and nature in her art reflect life-long attitudes which she expressed with conviction. They are themes that appeal to people today who share her concerns yet who are not interested in art. But the relevance of her work is widened in a way that would not have displeased her, for Emily Carr disliked a narrow aesthetic response.

Similarly, the changing view of social history brought about by the women's movement emphasizes her singular achievement. Probably she deserves a place in the history of that movement, for though there is nothing to suggest that she was, or would have wanted to be, an advance crusader for it, she did commit her life totally to her art at a time when women were normally confined to domestic roles. The degree to which her avoidance of the roles of lover, wife or mother stem from the commitment is a matter for conjecture, but the fact of the commitment and its results remain.

One statement she made, in addition to several passing comments, showed that she was well aware of the commonly held attitude towards women in her field. In mid-April of 1937 she received favourable reviews for a solo exhibition held in Toronto; she had also had recent sales that added up to an unprecedented $1,005. As usual she had to suppress her satisfaction (what if she should get smug?), but she was learning how to handle such good news: "I have dodged publicity, hated write-ups and all that splutter. Well, that's all selfish conceit that embarrassed me. I have been forgetting Canada and forgetting women painters. It's them I ought to be upholding, nothing to do with puny me at all. . . . I am also glad that I am showing these men that women can hold up their end. The men resent a woman getting any honour in what they consider is essentially their field. Men painters mostly despise women painters. So I have decided to stop squirming, to throw any honour in with Canada and women. It is wonderful to feel the grandness of Canada in the raw, not because she is Canada but because she's the something sublime that you were born into."[3]

Even the term "regional," which has been applied to Carr's work as if to diminish its value, is regarded differently today. In western society, with its centralization and control and its dependence on technology and instant information, power and prestige are seen to be located at the urban centre where life presumably is at its most concentrated and vital — where one is in touch. Today the consequences of the ideologies of modern societies, including the reckless exploitation of natural resources and the breaking of man's deep bond with nature, are becoming apparent. The sameness of goods, places and people is the new universality. Such ideologies are being challenged and revalued, and real advantages are being discovered in regionalism. Regionalists can dig deeper into the cultural deposits of their region, with more freedom for individuality and intensity, and can more easily affect their cultural climate. In this respect, Carr's regionalism also must be reassessed.

Once Carr was into her mature work, from the beginning of the 1930s, favourable critical attention was not lacking, even in the west coast papers, though there it was minimal and mainly journalistic. Reputations in art are still not made in Canada's West, and eastern criticism of Carr's work, though generous, often reflected the blunted vision of those at the centre who see outsiders as being limited by their provincial sources. Some who took a broader view could see her among the second generation who followed the lead of the Group of Seven and therefore as already a little out-of-date. For though she was a contemporary of its members in age, she met them when their originating impulse as a group was already playing out; and when she was hitting her full stride, newer energies, some of European and American origin, were asserting themselves in the Canadian art world. There was, for instance, the Kingston Conference of 1941, organized by Ontario artist André Bieler with the help of the National Gallery, an event of great importance for the country's artists, who had never before had the opportunity to meet together to discuss mutual problems. The idea of an art of social purpose was a familiar one — it had been debated in some Canadian art circles for at least five years — and this was a theme running through the conference, and discussed by guest speakers Thomas Hart Benton and E.P. Rowan, head of the American Works Program Administration.

By the forties, landscape painting in the Group of Seven spirit no longer engaged the progressive contemporary Canadian artist; Canadian art, as usual, was catching up on international art trends. Since then, whatever changes have taken place in cultural and critical attitudes, there has not been, till recently, the inclination to face the full force of Carr's heady and emotionally demanding individuality. In fact, it has only been in the seventies, as the hold of formalist-oriented criticism weakened and the stricture against interpretation was challenged, that Carr has come to be seen and valued for what she is.

Carr's last ten painting years released the romantic side of her nature. This is not to say that she was the simple romantic she is sometimes thought to be; in working her way through certain early twentieth-century painting attitudes and disciplines, and using the techniques involved, she had confirmed the intellectual tradition of her time. Still — and fortunately for her — she had no inclination to appropriate what she could not understand intuitively or what she could not adapt to her own purposes. She was not a theorizing artist or an innovator, but she knew where her own strengths lay.

An address that Carr gave in Victoria in 1930 briefly refers to Cézanne and quotes from Wilenski's *Modern Movement in Art*. Looked at as statements of aesthetics, her views of art appear simplistic, characteristically homespun in expression, revealing no intellectual grasp of the sweep, complexity or historical import of what had been going on in the world of art. Nonetheless her appeal for tolerance of "modern art" is passionate and rings true, for it is based on her own hard-won conviction. Modern art for her was less a movement to be understood than an issue to be faced, and more than anything, being on the side of modern art was taking a moral stand; it was being for life and against deadening convention, which was consistent with her life stance. The art books she read were often theoretical treatises that provided her with moral and philosophical arguments to support her intuitive convictions as to the importance of modern art, as distinct from those books of visual reference that told what other artists were doing.

Carr liked to have art-talk with sympathetic friends, but she would shut it off abruptly if it took an analytical turn, for she felt that analysis was antithetical to the nature of art. Also, she was uncomfortable in the realm of art theory because she felt that she was inarticulate. In November 1933 she was looking forward to a visit with her Toronto friends but with uneasiness: "I expect I shall only be able to sit like a bell without a tongue and just make a note if someone kicks me. I don't get much chance to talk to people out home about the real things, so I have no words. . . . I'm afraid to give out the little I have got, afraid of mixing things up and putting them wrong and being laughed at."[4] Again, in a letter to Eric Brown in 1937: "I wish I was better at talking. It is very difficult for me, I can't find what I want to say in books and copy it out because lots of it I don't believe and lots I don't understand and lots doesn't interest me."[5]

Emily Carr was an individual who did not sit comfortably in close company. Like any artist, she drew on whatever art sources were available to her, but she was never truly in step with any group, movement, or trend. She was inspired by the strong fresh look and the vigorous nationalist sentiment of the Group of Seven. She did not, however, adopt their painting conventions and she was fundamentally different from them in the degree to which she finally made her work the vehicle of feeling, and in the strong mystical tendency she shared with Harris alone. For a brief time she used a cubist-derived form system in her painting, though Cubism, as a formalist attitude, was not related to her goals, neither in 1911 when she could have witnessed some of its early experiments in Paris, nor in the late twenties when cubist practice could have reached her second-hand through Tobey or, in still more modified form, through Harris.

Carr repeatedly acknowledges her debt to Harris, and briefly to Tobey, but when she mentions international artists whose work she could have encountered on her travels or seen in books, they are usually passing references to an occasion rather than to their work.[6] And so the question of direct influence on her work remains mainly a matter of conjecture. The specific names her work evokes are more like spiritual but distant brothers or sisters whom she might not even recognize at first. Franz Marc is one such artist. His adaptation of the cubist mode to his own lyrical pantheism of the years 1911-13, expressed in shadowed woodsy interiors penetrated by shafts of light, was echoed in some of Carr's own forest interiors twenty years later. She certainly saw one of his paintings in a private collection in New York in 1930, and could have seen reproductions elsewhere, but perhaps the affinity is one of temperamental coincidence and of a common reference to the cubist style and has no other connection.

So too Georgia O'Keeffe, Carr's American contemporary, younger by sixteen years, to whose original and powerful statement Carr's work offers an intriguing parallel.

They met in the Stieglitz Gallery in New York on the same trip during which she saw Franz Marc's painting, and she liked some of O'Keeffe's work.

The landscapes of northern expressionist Edvard Munch are occasionally invoked in connection with Carr's work. And in certain of her paintings of the mid- and late-thirties, especially those with whirling skies, there is the superficial likeness to van Gogh. Several people pointed out the resemblance to her. But the correspondence, she claimed, was accidental. "I woke this morning with 'unity of movement' in a picture strong in my mind. I believe van Gogh [whose letters she was reading at the time] had that idea. I did not realize he had striven for that till quite recently so I did not come by the idea through him."[7]

Still, because of the quality of Carr's painting and its originality, such affinities are bound to suggest themselves and to hint at a larger relationship with other artists whose strength, like hers, grew out of isolation, particularly an inner isolation. Perhaps too they suggest audiences for her work outside Canada, for thus far her exposure abroad has been infrequent and has usually been confined to Canadian Government presentations.

In its overall content and character, Carr's work derives ultimately from an imaginative and cultural mode that was waning, not advancing — that of European nineteenth-century nature romanticism which had re-emerged in a Canadian form with the Group of Seven. They, before her, attached sentiments of spirituality and ethical value to nature, but in their painting they tended to concentrate on decorative visual effects, whereas she made her art the vehicle of intense personal emotion. Seeing her in this larger perspective, it is her distinction that she was able to achieve such a degree of vitality and authenticity while working within a tradition that had almost lost its collective animus.

CARR'S "REAL SUCCESS"   The pattern of Emily Carr's career, with its delayed start and late fulfillment, has a drama that lends lustre to her achievement. Her tardy beginning was different from that of fellow-Canadian Tom Thomson, who, though a commercial artist, had not thought of being a serious painter until he was thirty-five. Carr, beginning in her teens, sought and obtained appropriate training for an artist of her time, including study in an academic art school and two trips abroad. When, at the age of forty-one, she had her first exhibition of paintings in the highly sophisticated postimpressionist style, she could have been presumed to have launched her career and to be on her way. But something was not mixing properly in the complex chemistry of hand, eye, head and heart, and for almost a decade and a half, her art, while kept alive, went nowhere.

It is true that she had already located, through prolonged experience of them, the thematic areas through which her art was to be channeled: "The wild places and primitive people claimed me."[8] Yet it was not until she was in her late fifties that she learned to put these two areas of experience fully into the service of her art, when she came to understand the Indian's carvings as the expression of his experience in a primordial environment and was led in turn to a bolder perception of the forests and coastal landscape. When she finally was able to identify the primal energy she found in nature with the spiritual energy she was seeking as the manifestation of God, the elements in her art became integrated at a higher level. She was aware of this funda-mental change in herself and the new potency it gave her work. At this point her art reached its full range of effectiveness.

Carr is in the strongest sense regional. In one sense those forests, the carvings in their settings, giant trees, sea and beaches did not exist until she painted them. She gave form to a Pacific mythos, a form so carefully distilled in her imagination that even though we never visit the West Coast, we know it.

Her art was also an expression of her view of the world as life-energy, and from this point of view, west coast nature becomes the vehicle which manifests and symbolizes the "force beyond." Her conception of nature's energy, like that of Walt Whitman, from whose poetry she derived daily sustenance, is large in scale; her imagery deals with the force that drives forests to sea edge, that explodes the sky into a firmament, that makes of the undergrowth a rushing sea, that unifies creation as one living, moving energy. Her liberated psyche could deal with all aspects of that energy, from dark and devouring to rapturous and ecstatic.

For Carr, such a vitalistic view was comprehensible only in religious terms. The equation was: God equals vital principle. Her search for religious fulfillment was a powerful drive that found expression in her art. "Go out there into the glory of the woods. See God in every particle of them expressing glory and strength and power, tenderness and protection. Know that they are God expressing God made manifest. . . . It is a continuous process of life, eternally changing yet eternally the same. See God in it all, enter into the life of the trees."[9] Carr's talent was sufficient, though not exceptional; it was her vision that was grand. Robert Browning was one of her favourite poets, so the point can be made, using his words, that her reach always exceeded her grasp. It was her ceaseless struggle to bring her talent into the service of her vision that kept her sentiment from being banal and her paint brush from losing touch with her sense of what was real.

In reaching for worthy moral sentiments, as she often does in her writing, Carr speaks out of the prevailing ideology of her time. When she expresses herself in a religious terminology that meshes uncomfortably with our twentieth-century sensibilities, her thoughts and feelings can seem extravagant and excessive. But such sentiments are transformed and absorbed in her painting. We look at her art and we know what she meant. She paints a tree, a beach, a sky that invokes all trees, all growth, all space, all light and all dark. By virtue of her artistry and the imaginative enlargement of her themes, the best of her creations are universal. Her prolonged contact and empathy with one segment of the world's skin has led her to touch the pulse that animates the whole. In this sense her art exists as a metaphor for the larger cosmic energy that animates man and his world alike, binding them into one common universe.

This is what she sought: "Real success . . . to feel down in your own soul that the thing you have striven for has been accomplished."[10]

In the following list of reproductions dimensions are given in centimetres, and height precedes width. Established titles for paintings have been used, even when an Indian name following Carr's inscription is misspelled or does not follow current usage. Otherwise, the spelling of Indian names follows the usage of the Department of Ethnology, Provincial Museum of British Columbia. In the case of the many untitled works, a description is provided for identification purposes. Quotations from Carr's Journals, *Hundreds and Thousands*, have been indicated by the abbreviation HT.

The author has proposed dates for works undated by Carr, who was, by her own admission, careless about such things as dates, signatures and titles. Her lack of interest in the documentary side of art may have been affirmed by her reading of Clive Bell, who in his book *Art* speaks of the irrelevance of art history to art's appreciation. Lawren Harris recommended the book to her in 1927, and after 1929 she dated very few paintings. Indeed, in a letter to Ira Dilworth (in the Public Archives of Canada), probably in 1942, when she was tired of being pressed for catalogue data for her large exhibition at the Art Gallery of Toronto in 1943, she exploded: "I don't know one date in my life. I had no *periods* that I know of nor any direct planning of *how* I was going to or did work. I just *went on*, the other stuff is all jargon — when art sinks to jargon it's dead. Art should grow and become just as cabbage heads up. . . . I only named pictures because it was necessary when they went out to exhibition for catalogues. . . . I'm not a museum and I *won't* be a *datery*."

Anchor points for a chronology after 1929 can be established by a few exceptions to her habitual omission, such as *Loggers' Culls* of 1935 and the 1936 paintings *Reforestation* and *Shoreline*. To these canvases may be added several dated oil-on-paper sketches, as well as those from her last sketching session at Mount Douglas Park in 1942 — for in her last years she acceded, at least at times, to the demands of those concerned with exhibiting and promoting her work. It was at the urging of Dr. Max Stern that in 1944 she got busy and signed a backlog of accumulated work in her studio. Still, the problems facing anyone attempting to date the vast numbers of her undated works are considerable. Carr's major outdoor sketching trips from 1931 on can be charted from journals and correspondence, and sometimes subject matter can be identified with her working areas when a topographical feature identifies a particular locale (though what about the ubiquitous trees?). Her general stylistic evolution is observable as well as stylistic mannerisms which connect groups of works; but, like other artists, she also had overlapping or back-tracking style habits. Exhibiting records can be of help, but many works were never shown publicly, particularly sketches. Those that were can often not be identified in exhibition lists because different works were frequently given similar or identical titles, and sometimes titles were changed either by Carr in forgetfulness or by someone else. Evidence from her Journals and correspondence offer fragmentary evidence at best.

By correlating the data from various sources, certain works may be dated with reasonable certainty. But many have had to be given approximate dates, particularly the many oil-on-paper paintings. Exhibition records are referred to only when they have a possible bearing on dates.

SUNSHINE AND TUMULT

1 oil on paper 87.0 x 57.1 cm, signed lower left: *EMILY CARR* [c.1938-39]
The Art Gallery of Hamilton, bequest of H.S. Southam

This sketch appears on the easel in the background of Harold Mortimer Lamb's photograph of Carr. The painting was exhibited in her solo exhibition at the Vancouver Art Gallery, November 1939 ($50). In its handling of foliage as rippling ribbons of pigment, it resembles *Tree Boles in September*, a more "finished" sketch that was shown in the same exhibition.

TOTEM AND FOREST

◁ 2 oil on canvas 128.8 x 55.9 cm, signed lower right: *M. EMILY CARR* [1931]
The Vancouver Art Gallery

The pole depicted was originally a house pole of the house belonging to the Edenshaw family at Tow Hill, Queen Charlotte Islands. Carr could have seen it there, or after 1923 when it was removed to Prince Rupert where it stood for many years. Today it is in the Prince Rupert Museum. A photo in the *Provincial Museum of British Columbia* (PN 11.36) and another in Barbeau's *Totem Poles* (vol. 1, p. 210), show it against a forest background, as does this canvas. There is a likely reference to it in Carr's Journal entry on 28 January 1931: "I was working on a big totem with heavy woods behind" (HT, p. 25), which together with its stylistic character suggest the date. There is also the fact that it was exhibited in March of that year with the Ontario Society of Artists exhibition in Toronto.

ALICE CARR

3 watercolour 44.5 x 34.6 cm, signed and dated lower left: *M. EMILY CARR. 1909*
private collection

Alice, Emily's schoolteacher sister, was her favourite.

ROCK BAY BRIDGE, VICTORIA

4 ink 16.1 x 22.5 cm, signed and dated lower left: *M. Carr/Aug. 2nd, 1895*; inscribed lower right: *Rock Bay Bridge*
Newcombe Collection, Provincial Archives of British Columbia

A similar drawing, dated the same day but without the North Ward School in the background, is in a private collection.

GIANT TREES, STANLEY PARK (Vancouver)

5 oil on wood 63.5 x 47.6 cm, signed and dated lower right: *M CARR 1909*
private collection

One of several known versions of this subject; two watercolours are in the collection of the Vancouver Art Gallery.

PORTRAIT OF A CHILD

6 carbon pencil 38.1 x 32.1 cm, signed lower left (script): *M Carr* [1890]
private collection

According to the present owner it was done before, or just a few months after, Carr's enrollment in the California School of Design in San Francisco. The subject is a child of Carr's guardian, J.H. Lawson. It was probably done from a photograph, as were other similar portrait drawings of children of family or friends done around this time.

Meadow with arbutus (untitled)

7 watercolour 34.3 x 50.8 cm, signed and dated lower right: *M. EMILY CARR. 1909*
private collection

CEDAR CANNIBAL HOUSE, UCLUELET, B.C.

8 watercolour 17.9 x 26.5 cm, signed and inscribed lower right: *M CARR/UCLUELET B.C.* [1898]
Newcombe Collection, Provincial Archives of British Columbia

Carr's first known sketches of an Indian settlement were done at Ucluelet, Vancouver Island, on a visit in 1898.

SKAGWAY

9 watercolour 26.4 x 35.7 cm, signed lower right (red): *M. CARR*
inscribed on reverse: *Skagway from end of wharf — cold wind. Ugh! August 1907*
Newcombe Collection, Provincial Archives of British Columbia

BRITTANY LANDSCAPE

10 oil on gessoed card 44.1 x 61.3 cm, signed lower right: *M. EMILY CARR* [1911]
private collection

The information that this is one of Carr's two paintings exhibited in the *Salon d'Automne* exhibition in Paris, 1911, was given by the artist to Dr. Max Stern of the Dominion Gallery in Montreal, who sold the painting to its present owner. The catalogue entries for Carr's paintings in that exhibition were no. 245, *La Colline*, and no. 246, *Le Paysage.*

AUTUMN IN FRANCE

11 oil on board 50.2 x 66.1 cm, signed lower right: *M. EMILY CARR* [1911]
The National Gallery of Canada

BRITTANY KITCHEN

12 oil on card 51.2 x 66 cm, signed lower right: *M. EMILY CARR* [1911]
private collection

OLD CHURCH NEAR ST. EFFLAM

13 oil on card 41.3 x 33.7 cm, signed lower right: *M CARR* [1912]
Fannin Hall Collection Ltd., Vancouver

CONCARNEAU

14 watercolour 26.4 x 35.9 cm, signed, inscribed and dated lower right (script):
Emily Carr/ Concarneau 1911
Dr. and Mrs. Max Stern, Dominion Gallery, Montreal

ALERT BAY

15 oil on canvas 61 x 92.3 cm, signed lower left: *M. E. CARR/ALERT BAY* [1912 or early 1913]
private collection

SKETCH FOR INDIAN VILLAGE OF ALERT BAY

◁ watercolour 48.1 x 83.5 cm, signed lower right: *EMILY CARR*; dated (on reverse): *1908*
inscribed lower right: *Rough Sketch for Indian Village of Alert Bay, B.C.*
Newcombe Collection, Provincial Archives of British Columbia

The paper has been joined.

WAR CANOES (Alert Bay)

16 watercolour 36.9 x 48.9 cm, signed lower right (red and black): *M. CARR* [c.1908]
private collection

WAR CANOES (Alert Bay)

17 oil on canvas 63.5 x 80 cm, signed and dated lower right: *M. EMILY CARR 1912*
private collection

SKIDEGATE

18 oil on board 65.4 x 32.5 cm, signed, inscribed and dated lower left: *M EMILY CARR/ SKIDIGATE 1912*
The Vancouver Art Gallery

This painting is reproduced in Marius Barbeau, *Totem Poles*, vol. 2, p. 491. Compare with 1928 painting of same pole, no. 40.

TZARTSISEUCOMY (Tsatsisnukwomi)

19 watercolour 54.7 x 75.6 cm, signed lower left and inscribed: *M E CARR/ TZARTSISEUCOMY* [c.1912]
Dr. and Mrs. Max Stern, Dominion Gallery, Montreal

A dated watercolour indicates that Carr visited the southern Kwakiutl village of Tsatsisnukwomi (New Vancouver) as early as 1909. However, the decorative rhythms in the foreground of this painting suggest a 1912 date.

TSATSINUCHOMI B.C. (Tsatsisnukwomi)

20 watercolour 55.9 x 77.1 cm, signed and inscribed lower right: *EMILY CARR/ Tsatsinuchomi B.C.* [c.1912]
The Vancouver Art Gallery

This watercolour and its companion in the National Gallery of Canada represent inside posts of a
a house in the southern Kwakiutl village of Tsatsisnukwomi. They appear also in the canvas
Indian House Interior with Totems.

HOUSE POST, TSATSISNUKWOMI, B.C.

21 watercolour 53.4 x 75.7 cm, unsigned [c.1912]
The National Gallery of Canada

This watercolour was among the paintings that Carr sent to Ottawa in the fall of 1927; it was purchased by the National Gallery in 1929. Until recently it has borne the incorrect identification "Tanoo."

TANOO, QUEEN CHARLOTTE ISLANDS

22 oil on canvas 110.5 x 170.8 cm, signed, dated and inscribed, lower right: M. EMILY CARR/ TANOO Q.C.I. 1913
Provincial Archives of British Columbia

Tanoo was a Haida village on Moresby Island, one of the Queen Charlotte group.

MEMALILAQUA, KNIGHT'S INLET

23 oil on canvas 130.2 x 89.2 cm, signed lower right: M. EMILY CARR [1912 or early 1913]
The National Gallery of Canada

See note on the following related watercolour; Mamalillikulla is actually the name of the people, Mimquimlees the village where this house was located. Note Carr's addition of the figures in the canvas version.

CEDAR HOUSE STAIRCASE AND SUNBURST

24 watercolour 70.7 x 56.1 cm, signed lower right: EMILY CARR; inscribed lower right: Tribe Klowakis/Village Karlukwees [1912]
Newcombe Collection, Provincial Archives of British Columbia

Carr's identification inscription is incorrect. The location is the southern Kwakiutl village of Mimquimlees on Village Island.

GUISDOMS

25 watercolour 54 x 74.3 cm, signed and inscribed lower left: M.E. CARR/ GUISDOMS [1912]
private collection

Gwayasdums is a southern Kwakiutl village on Gilford Island near Alert Bay. Carr discussed her 1912 visit to this village in her lecture on totem poles given at the time of her 1913 exhibition of Indian paintings in Vancouver.

INDIAN HOUSE INTERIOR WITH TOTEMS

26 oil on canvas 89.5 x 130.5 cm, unsigned [1912 or early 1913]
The Vancouver Art Gallery

See notes on the related watercolours, nos. 20 and 21. A Newcombe photograph in the Provincial Museum, Victoria, taken in 1900, shows the interior of this Kwakiutl house intact, though by 1923 it was gone. In 1912 Carr could probably have seen it in its undeteriorated state. The foreground of this painting appears unfinished, possibly overpainted and left unresolved — a compositional area that is sometimes awkwardly handled in her work. The absence of signature confirms the view that it is unfinished.

ARBUTUS TREE

27 oil on canvas 45.9 x 35.6 cm, signed and dated lower right: M E CARR/1922
private collection

The painterly assertion of negative areas between branches and the breaks in foliage show how well Carr had absorbed her postimpressionist lesson. It also shows that she was aware of the problem of the inter-relationship of sky and trees long before she commented on it in June 1935 (HT, p. 132).

Clump of trees against whirling sky (untitled)

◁ 27a oil on canvas 57.2 x 48.3 cm, estate stamp lower left [c.1913-15]
private collection

This painting resembles several others that bear titles relating them to Beacon Hill Park. The use of separate, directional brush strokes, which contribute to a larger pictorial movement (as in *Autumn in France*, 1911) rather than spread patches of pigment (as in *Arbutus Tree*, 1922), suggest a date early rather than late in the decade.

SAWMILLS, VANCOUVER

28 oil on gessoed canvas 35.9 x 45.4 cm, signed lower right: M.E. CARR [1912 or 1913]
Dr. and Mrs. Max Stern, Dominion Gallery, Montreal

Carr had a studio at 1465 West Broadway, Vancouver, from early 1912 to mid-1913.

ALONG THE CLIFF, BEACON HILL (Victoria)

29 oil on card 37.6 x 45.3 cm, signed and dated lower right: *M. EMILY CARR/ 1919*
private collection

There are at least two other paintings of this period similar to this one in subject and in the broad,
coarse handling of pigment — one in the Glenbow Museum, Calgary, and the other in a
private collection.

VANCOUVER STREET

30 oil on card 18.4 x 22.9 cm, signed lower left (black): *M CARR*; signed lower right (white): *EMILY CARR*
[1912 or early 1913]
private collection

Carr told the present owner, who purchased the painting in 1941, that she thought the subject was
Broadway Street where she had her studio.

QUEEN CHARLOTTE ISLANDS TOTEM

31 watercolour 76.2 x 53.8 cm, signed, inscribed and dated lower right: *M EMILY CARR/ Q.C.I. 1928*
The Vancouver Art Gallery

The subject appears to be the lower part of a pole at Gold Harbour (also known as Haina or Xaina).

KISPIOX VILLAGE

32 watercolour 76.5 x 53.7 cm, signed lower right: *M. EMILY CARR* [1928]
The Vancouver Art Gallery

A 1912 canvas of this same subject, now in a private collection, was originally purchased by Marius
Barbeau and is reproduced in his *Downfall of Temlahan*.

MAUD ISLAND TOTEMS, QUEEN CHARLOTTE ISLANDS

33 watercolour 76.2 x 56.8 cm, signed and inscribed lower left: *M. EMILY CARR/MAUD ISLAND Q.C.I.* [1928]
The Vancouver Art Gallery

Totem pole with geometrically stylized foliage (untitled)

34 watercolour 75.9 x 28.1 cm, signed lower right: *M. Emily Carr* [c.1928-29]
The Vancouver Art Gallery

Shown is a Tsimshian pole from Angidah on the lower Nass River, which is now in the Royal Ontario
Museum.

KITWANCOOL

35 watercolour 75.9 x 56.5 cm, signed lower left: *EMILY CARR*; inscribed lower left (pencil): *Kitwancool*
[c.1928]
The Vancouver Art Gallery

The developed conceptual character indicates that this is a studio watercolour.

THE GREAT EAGLE, SKIDEGATE B.C.

36 watercolour 73.7 x 53.4 cm, signed lower left (script): *M. EMILY CARR* [1929]
private collection

Exhibited October 1929 in Victoria at the Island Arts and Crafts Society exhibition (no. 81, $75).

SKIDEGATE

◁ oil on card 64.5 x 32.4 cm, signed, inscribed and dated lower right: *M. EMILY CARR/SKIDIGATE 1912*
The Vancouver Art Gallery

Compare with the 1928-29 watercolour of the same subject.

BRITISH COLUMBIA INDIAN VILLAGE

37 oil on canvas 111.8 x 71 cm, signed lower left: *M. EMILY CARR* [1930]
The Vancouver Art Gallery

On 23 November 1930 Carr worked on a charcoal drawing of Fort Rupert and on 24 November she
"tried the thing on canvas" (HT, p. 21). In December 1930 she was hurrying to finish the "Baltimore
canvas" (HT, p. 23). The references are to this canvas, which was exhibited in the First Baltimore
Pan-American Exhibition early in 1931 under the title *British Columbia Indian Village*. It is probably
also the painting shown under the title *Indian Village, B.C.* in the National Gallery's Annual
Exhibition in January-February 1931. Like *Vanquished* and *Big Raven* this painting combines
a geometrically structured sky with "fluid" foliage, and like them it was painted after her visit in
the spring of 1930 to Toronto and New York. Had she not already demonstrated this structural mode
in 1928 and 1929 paintings, one would look for sources of influence stemming from that trip.

KITWANCOOL

38 oil on canvas 101.3 x 83.2 cm, signed lower left: *M. EMILY CARR* [spring 1928]
The Glenbow Museum, Calgary

A sticker on the stretcher and a faint brush inscription on the canvas back say "June 9, 1928." This is therefore almost certainly the painting exhibited in the Group of Seven Toronto exhibition of April 1930 under the curious title *June 9, 1928*. In October 1928 Carr exhibited a painting *Kitwincool Northern B.C.* with the Island Arts and Crafts Society in Victoria (no. 79, $200), which might be this canvas or the one in the collection of Hart House, University of Toronto. In any case, Carr did not actually visit Kitwancool village until the summer of 1928. See text pp. 70, 72.

THE CRYING TOTEM

39 oil on canvas 74.9 x 38.8 cm, signed lower right: *M. EMILY CARR* [1928]
The Vancouver Art Gallery

The subject is a pole from Tanoo in the Queen Charlotte Islands. A replica stands in the courtyard of the Provincial Museum in Victoria, B.C. For a note on the date see text p. 70.

SKIDEGATE

40 oil on canvas 61 x 45.5 cm, signed lower left: *M EMILY CARR* [1928]
The Vancouver Art Gallery

For a note on the date see text p. 70.

◁ Photograph of Xaina (Heina) by R. Maynard, 1884
courtesy of Ethnology Division, Provincial Museum of British Columbia

HEINA, Q.C.I.

41 watercolour 75.6 x 56.2 cm, signed lower right: *EMILY CARR*; inscribed on reverse: *Heina Q.C.I. from a photograph* (pencil)
Newcombe Collection, Provincial Archives of British Columbia

The inscription does not appear to be in Carr's hand and may be that of "Willie" Newcombe.

HEINA, Q.C.I.

42 oil on canvas 129.5 x 91.4 cm, signed lower right, inscribed and dated: *M EMILY CARR/ Q.C.I. 1928*
The National Gallery of Canada

This Haida village (also known as Gold Harbour) was no longer inhabited when Carr visited it. The painting was worked out from an 1884 photograph by Maynard, and a recent X-ray of the canvas shows an underpainting much closer to the photograph than the finished work. *Totem Village*, a canvas very similar in style, in the collection of the Vancouver Art Gallery, was also developed from a photo at this same time.

KISPIOX

43 watercolour 75.9 x 55.6 cm, signed lower right: *EMILY CARR*; inscribed upper left: *Kispiox* [1928]
The Vancouver Art Gallery

THREE TOTEMS (Kispiox)

44 oil on canvas 108 x 68.6 cm, signed lower left: *M.E. CARR* [1928]
The Vancouver Art Gallery

The dry handling of paint and the treatment of the central background pole is very similar to that in *Kitwancool*, no. 38.

VANQUISHED

45 oil on canvas 92.1 x 128.9 cm, signed lower left: *M EMILY CARR* [probably 1931]
The Vancouver Art Gallery

The location is the old Haida village of Skedans, Queen Charlotte Islands, which Carr visited in 1912 and again in 1928. The similarity of this canvas in style and mood to *Big Raven* suggests that this is one of the Indian canvases done in the spring of 1931. She wrote in her Journal, "I want to paint some skies so that they look roomy and moving and mysterious and to make them overhang the earth, to have a different quality in their distant horizon and their overhanging nearness." (HT, p. 28) Exhibited in Amsterdam in 1933 at Stedelijk Museum, International Federation of Business and Professional Women, Exhibition of Works by Women Artists organized by the International Committee of Fine Arts.

THE RAVEN (Maud Island, Haina, Q.C.I.)

46   oil on canvas 61 x 45.7 cm, signed lower left: M E CARR [1928 or 1929]
     private collection
     Exhibited with the British Columbia Society of Fine Arts, Vancouver, November 1929, confirming
     a 1928 or 1929 dating.

Top of a pole at Gold Harbour

◁   watercolour 19.4 x 16.5 cm, estate stamp lower left; inscribed on reverse: *Maude Island*
     Newcombe Collection, Provincial Archives of British Columbia
     See photographs of this pole in Barbeau, *Totem Poles*, vol. 2, pp. 495-96. Represented is the Raven
     holding a copper shield in his beak.

CUMSHEWA

47   watercolour 51.4 x 74.3 cm, signed and inscribed lower left: *M.E. CARR / CUMSHEWA* [c.1912]
     The National Gallery of Canada
     Almost certainly a studio watercolour developed from first-hand material done on a 1912 visit to
     this abandoned Haida village in the Queen Charlotte Islands. Carr planned to visit here again in the
     summer of 1928 but managed only a brief emergency stop in Cumshewa Inlet during a storm.

BIG RAVEN

48   oil on canvas 86.7 x 113.8 cm, signed lower right: *M. EMILY CARR* [1931]
     The Vancouver Art Gallery
     The date is based on a 5 February 1931 entry in her Journals: "Got the Cumshewa big bird well
     disposed on canvas. The great bird is on a post in tangled growth, a distant mountain below and
     a lowering, heavy sky and one pine tree. I want to bring great loneliness to this canvas and a haunting
     broodiness, quiet and powerful." (HT, p. 27)

KWAKIUTL

49   watercolour 26.4 x 35.7 cm, estate stamp lower left and on reverse [1909-12]
     Newcombe Collection, Provincial Archives of British Columbia
     Location is the southern Kwakiutl village of Mimquimlees, Village Island, B.C.

POTLATCH FIGURE

50   oil on canvas 44.5 x 59.7 cm, signed lower right: *EMILY CARR* [1912]
     Dr. and Mrs. Max Stern, Dominion Gallery, Montreal

POTLATCH WELCOME

51   oil on canvas 110.3 x 67.2 cm, signed lower left: *M E CARR* [1930-31]
     The Art Gallery of Ontario, bequest of Charles S. Band
     The relatively fluid handling of foliage suggests a date after 1928-29.

KITWA[N]COOL TOTEMS

52   oil on canvas 105.4 x 68.3 cm, signed, inscribed and dated lower left: *M. EMILY CARR/ KITWACOOL 1928*
     Hart House, University of Toronto

TOTEM MOTHER, KITWANCOOL

53   oil on canvas 109.2 x 69.3 cm, signed lower right: *M. EMILY CARR* [1928]
     The Vancouver Art Gallery
     Exhibited October 1928, in the Victoria Island Arts and Crafts Society exhibition, which confirms
     the 1928 date.

INDIAN HUT, QUEEN CHARLOTTE ISLANDS

54   oil on canvas 101.6 x 81.9 cm, signed lower left: *M. E. CARR* [c.1930]
     The National Gallery of Canada, The Vincent Massey Bequest
     Like other canvases of its time, this is a composite work. The poles are from the village of Cumshewa,
     which was abandoned when Carr visited it in 1912, and Carr places them behind the Indian house,
     rather than in front as they actually were.

GUYASDOMS' D'SONOQUA

55   oil on canvas 100.3 x 65.4 cm, signed lower left: *M. EMILY CARR* [1929-30]
     The Art Gallery of Ontario
     Carr describes her 1912 visit to the Kwakiutl village Gwayasdums, on Gilford Island, in an April
     1913 lecture on Totem Poles (Public Archives of Canada). She and the young Indian girl who

accompanied her "were the only living creatures in the place with the exception of a poor half-mad dog." Gwayasdums, unlike Alert Bay some eighteen miles distant, was "off the beaten track . . . one of the old-time original villages, unchanged by fashion and civilization. . . . The fronts of these houses are truly imposing, solid hand hewn cedar planks some inches thick, posts and beams enormous." A watercolour sketch for this canvas is in the Newcombe Collection, Victoria. This is the first of three carved figures she describes in the story "D'Sonoqua" in *Klee Wyck* (p. 33).

KOSKIMO

56 watercolour 75.9 x 56.7 cm, signed lower right: *EMILY CARR* [1930]
The Vancouver Art Gallery

See note for *Zunoqua of the Cat Village*. The central carving here represents a D'Sonoqua with the mouth characteristically open in the position of uttering her cry. The spontaneous handling of the watercolour suggests that this is an on-location sketch. In an unpublished notebook in the Public Archives of Canada, headed "Cat Village," September 1930, Carr describes working at this location for two days, from 9 a.m. to 6 p.m.

ZUNOQUA OF THE CAT VILLAGE

57 oil on canvas 112.2 x 70.6 cm, signed lower right: *M. E. CARR* [1931]
The Vancouver Art Gallery

This and the other two reproduced works dealing with the cat-village theme are based on a visit to the Kwakiutl village of Quattiche in Quatsino Sound, Vancouver Island, late summer 1930, which Carr describes in the story "D'Sonoqua" in *Klee Wyck* (pp. 38-40) and in unpublished Journal entries in the Public Archives of Canada. She worked on the material from this visit in February 1931 (see HT, p. 26). Carr mistakenly identifies the carving in this painting as D'Sonoqua, the cannibal woman of Indian mythology, though she correctly describes its original function as an inside house pole. This is the third of the three poles she describes in that story.

KOSKIMO

◁ 58 charcoal on paper 77.9 x 56.2 cm, unsigned [1930]
The Vancouver Art Gallery

See notes for previous painting. The completed character of this drawing and its closeness to the canvas suggest that it is a studio drawing, probably done in the fall of 1930.

STRANGLED BY GROWTH

59 oil on canvas 63.5 x 48.3 cm, signed lower right: *M. EMILY CARR* [1931]
The Vancouver Art Gallery

See Carr's Journal entry, 1 February 1931: "I worked all afternoon, first on 'Koskemo Village,' X.I., and then on X.2., 'Strangled by Growth,' which is also Koskemo [the cat village]." (HT, p. 26)

KITWANGAR POLE

60 oil on canvas 68.9 x 57.3 cm, signed lower left: *M. EMILY CARR* [1929]
The Province of British Columbia, Provincial Archives

Kitwanga, a Tsimshian village in the Skeena River area of northern B.C. Exhibited October 1929 in the Island Arts and Crafts Society exhibition, Victoria.

TANOO

◁ 61 watercolour 74.9 x 52.7 cm, signed and inscribed lower left: *M.E. CARR/ TANOO* [1912]
Dr. and Mrs. Max Stern, Dominion Gallery, Montreal

The decorative handling of foreground growth, the outlining in blue of middle distance and distant trees, the touches of warm colour are all characteristic of the post-France date.

NIRVANA

62 oil on canvas 108.6 x 69.3 cm, signed lower right. *M EMILY CARR* [1929-30]
private collection

Exhibited with the Group of Seven exhibition in Toronto, April 1930, which indicates a 1929, or possibly early 1930 date. The title doubtless reflects Carr's interest at that time in theosophy, and its connections with near-Eastern thought.

BLUNDEN HARBOUR

63 oil on canvas 129.5 x 94.0 cm, signed lower left: *M. EMILY CARR* [1931 or 1932]
The National Gallery of Canada

This canvas was painted from a photograph of Blunden Harbour, a village which Carr never visited. The photograph was taken in 1901 by Dr. C.F. Newcombe, and lent to her around 1930. See *Emily*

Carr's "Blunden Harbour" by Maria Tippett, The National Gallery of Canada Bulletin no. 25, 1975; and *m.e.* by Edythe Hembroff-Schleicher, pp. 55-56. The photograph is reproduced in Barbeau's *Totem Poles*, vol. 2, p. 688, and in *Up and Down the North Pacific Coast by Canoe and Mission Ship*, by Rev. T. Crosby, Toronto, 1914.

THE WELCOME MAN

64   oil on card mounted on masonite 95.3 x 64.8 cm, signed, inscribed and dated lower right:
M. EMILY CARR/ KARLUKWEES B.C. 1913
The Art Emporium, Vancouver
The location is the Kwakiutl village of Kalokwis on Turnour Island.

SILHOUETTE NO. 2

65   oil on canvas 130.2 x 86 cm, signed lower right: *M. E. CARR*   [1930-31]
The Vancouver Art Gallery

SOUTH BAY, SKIDEGATE

66   watercolour 55.9 x 73.7 cm, signed lower right: *EMILY CARR*   [1928]
private collection
This is almost certainly one of the thirty large watercolours Carr did during her northern trip in the summer of 1928. It compares in handling with the *Queen Charlotte Islands Totem* watercolour, dated 1928.

OLD TIME COAST VILLAGE

67   oil on canvas 91.5 x 128.3 cm, signed lower left: *M. EMILY CARR*   [1929]
The Vancouver Art Gallery
This date is suggested on the basis of similarity of concept and style with *Indian Church*: placing of man's structures in contrast against nature's vast green strength; nature conceived as an impenetrable, frontally pressing wall with foliage as sculpted heavy slabs of plastic green.

South Bay, Skidegate (untitled)

◁ 68   oil on canvas 58.4 x 68.6 cm, signed lower right: *M. EMILY CARR*   [1929-30]
private collection; ex. coll. Marius Barbeau
In a Canadian Broadcasting Corporation recording, dated 1957, Barbeau recalled: "When I visited her in 1928, that is the year after the exhibition in Ottawa, I saw canvases with just trees, surrounded by skirts of ballet girls, or virgins of the forest, — densely green, but full of shapes and power. I couldn't resist buying one of them — mid-size." This is certainly the canvas referred to, though the more plastic character of the foliage compared to the chiselled handling of 1928 canvases suggests that his recollection is out by a year or so.

INDIAN CHURCH

69   oil on canvas 108.6 x 68.9 cm, signed lower right: *M. EMILY CARR*   [1929]
The Art Gallery of Ontario, bequest of Charles S. Band
The canvas was exhibited in November 1929 with the Island Arts and Crafts Society exhibition, confirming a 1929 date. Lawren Harris originally bought the painting and subsequently sold it to Charles Band on the condition that he would eventually give it to the Art Gallery of Toronto (later renamed the Art Gallery of Ontario).

Forest interior study (untitled)

70   oil on canvas, white gesso ground 59.4 x 36.3 cm, estate stamp lower left and on reverse [c.1929-30]
Newcombe Collection, Provincial Archives of British Columbia
One of several similar highly abstracted forest studies in the Newcombe Collection. The paint is thin and dry and there are areas of untouched canvas.

INSIDE A FOREST II

71   oil on canvas 109.9 x 69.8 cm, signed lower right: *M. EMILY CARR*   [c.1929-31]
The Art Gallery of Ontario, bequest of Charles S. Band

THE INDIAN CHURCH, FRIENDLY COVE

72   watercolour and charcoal on paper 59.1 x 45.1 cm, signed, dated and inscribed lower right:
EMILY CARR / 1929 / FRIENDLY COVE
The Art Emporium, Vancouver
This is one of several watercolours relating to the canvas *Indian Church* which were done on a trip to Friendly Cove, Nootka Sound, Vancouver Island in 1929.

PORT RENFREW
73 charcoal on paper 64.6 x 50.8 cm, unsigned [c.1929-30]
The Vancouver Art Gallery

WESTERN FOREST
74 oil on canvas 128.3 x 91.8 cm, signed lower right: *M EMILY CARR* [1929-30]
The Art Gallery of Ontario

This painting was exhibited as *Western Canadian Forest* in the Group of Seven exhibition, Toronto, April 1930.

WOOD INTERIOR
75 oil on canvas 106.68 x 69.9 cm, signed lower left: *M EMILY CARR.* [1929-30]
private collection

Exhibited with the Group of Seven exhibition in Toronto, April 1930 under the title *Forest* and in March 1932 at the Roerich Museum, New York under the above title. It was also in the exhibition, *Emily Carr, Her Paintings and Sketches* 1948, the National Gallery of Canada and the Art Gallery of Toronto, no. 39.

OLD TREE AT DUSK
76 oil on canvas 111.8 x 68.6 cm, signed lower right: *EMILY CARR* [c.1932]
The McMichael Canadian Collection, Kleinburg, Ontario

This painting does not appear, at least under its present title, in exhibition records until Carr's solo show at the Vancouver Art Gallery in November 1938, but with its strongly modelled forms and clear spatial structure it clearly belongs to the early years of the decade.

TREE
77 oil on canvas 129.2 x 56.2 cm, signed lower left: *M. EMILY CARR* [1931]
The Vancouver Art Gallery

In a letter to Carr dated 6 December 1931 (Public Archives of Canada), Lawren Harris speaks of her reference in a prior letter to her "tree trunk pictures." There are other paintings of this time in which Carr sees massive tree trunks as sensuous, tumescent, twisting columns (as in *Forest, British Columbia*) but none in which she deals with the subject so exclusively and abstractly as here.

FOREST, BRITISH COLUMBIA
78 oil on canvas 130 x 86.5 cm, signed lower right: *M EMILY CARR* [1931-32]
The Vancouver Art Gallery

OLD AND NEW FOREST
79 oil on canvas 111.8 x 69.5 cm, signed lower left: *M E CARR* [c.1931-32]
The Vancouver Art Gallery

This painting does not turn up in exhibiting records (at least not under this title) until 1937, when it was shown at the Canadian Group of Painters exhibition in Toronto; but its stylistic idioms — the hanging drape of foliage at the top, the solidly formed conical trees — call for an earlier date. Possibly the young foreground trees were repainted later.

INSIDE A FOREST I
◁ oil on paperboard 85.7 x 60.3 cm, signed lower left: *M EMILY CARR* [c.1930-31]
The Art Gallery of Ontario

THE LITTLE PINE
80 oil on canvas 111.6 x 68.7 cm, signed lower right: *M. E. CARR* [1931]
The Vancouver Art Gallery

This is probably the *Little Pine* exhibited in December 1931 with the Group of Seven's exhibition at the Art Gallery of Toronto; and also the one to which Lawren Harris referred in a letter of 6 December 1931 as "the little green yellow tree."

SEA DRIFT AT THE EDGE OF THE FOREST
81 oil on canvas 111.8 x 68.1 cm, signed lower left: *EMILY CARR* [1931]
The Vancouver Art Gallery

GREY

82 oil on canvas 106.7 x 68.9 cm, signed lower right: *M. E. CARR* [1931-32]
private collection

The motif of overlapping conical trees is seen also in *The Little Pine, Old Tree at Dusk*, and later in *Forsaken*. The chromatic concept of grey relates this painting to the group of sketches — oil-on-card or early oil-on-paper works — similarly carried out in ranges of grey, which she did around the same time.

Eye in the forest (untitled)

83 charcoal 62.7 x 47.9 cm, unsigned [1930-31]
The Vancouver Art Gallery

Young trees in wooded clearing (untitled)

84 charcoal on paper 62.6 x 48.1 cm, unsigned [1930-31]
The Vancouver Art Gallery

Formalized cedar (untitled)

85 charcoal on paper 92.7 x 61.4 cm, unsigned [1930-31]
The Vancouver Art Gallery

Cedar, horizontal (untitled)

86 charcoal on paper 30.3 x 46 cm, unsigned [1930-31]
The Vancouver Art Gallery

"Fish-eye lens" view of island (untitled)

87 charcoal on paper 47.9 x 62.2 cm, unsigned [1930-31]
The Vancouver Art Gallery

DESERTED VILLAGE

88 charcoal on paper 62 x 49.2 cm, unsigned, inscribed on reverse: *Highland District* [1930-31]
The Vancouver Art Gallery

DISTANT HILLSIDE

89 charcoal on paper 46 x 30 cm, unsigned [c.1932]
The Vancouver Art Gallery

FOREST LANDSCAPE

◁ 90 oil on paper 89 x 61.5 cm, signed lower right: *M E CARR* [1932]
private collection

Compare with the dated 1932 *Forest Interior*. The large-scale rhythms, broad, well-formed masses, and the well-covered paper indicate an early date for this oil-on-paper painting. It was probably done on Carr's May sketching trip to the Metchosin Hills in 1932.

Stylized trees (untitled)

91 oil on paper 87.9 x 61.1 cm, signed lower right: *M EMILY CARR* [1931-32]
The Vancouver Art Gallery

BRITISH COLUMBIA FOREST

92 oil on paper 91.4 x 61 cm, signed lower right: *M.E. CARR* [c.1931]
Dr. and Mrs. Max Stern, Dominion Gallery, Montreal

The touches of brown colour are the aging paper showing through thin areas of the paint. Stylistic similarities date it as belonging to the same period as *Forest, British Columbia* and *Deep Forest*.

Forest interior, black and grey (untitled)

93 oil on paper 89.4 x 60.7 cm, signed lower left: *M.E. CARR* [1931-32]
The Vancouver Art Gallery

B.C. FOREST

94 oil on paper 57.2 x 82.6 cm, signed and dated lower left: *M. EMILY CARR / 1934*
Galerie Royale, Vancouver

On 5 June 1934, while camping off Metchosin Road, Carr wrote in her Journals, "Sketched in the big old wood. Trees old-fashioned, broad-spreading and nobly moulded, beyond cutting age. There is no undergrowth in that wood, only old fallen branches and wild grass, but mostly moss, very deep and silent, sponging down many old secrets." (HT, p. 130).

ABSTRACT TREE FORMS
95 oil on paper 61 x 93.5 cm, signed lower right: *M E CARR*; signed lower left: *EMILY CARR* [1931-32]
The Vancouver Art Gallery

FOREST INTERIOR
96 oil on paper 90.8 x 60.3 cm, signed and dated lower left: *M. E. CARR, 1932*
private collection
This painting was signed at the time of purchase ($10) at the owner's request. Carr volunteered to date it as well, thus establishing one of the relatively few firm dates of this period.

At Beacon Hill Park (untitled)
97 oil on paper 60 x 90.8 cm, estate stamp lower left [c.1935]
private collection
This painting has sometimes carried the inappropriate title *The Wheat Field*.

SHORELINE
98 oil on canvas 68.6 x 111.7 cm, signed and dated lower left: *M. EMILY CARR 1936*
The McMichael Canadian Collection, Kleinburg, Ontario
This oil was exhibited in June 1936 at the Vancouver Art Gallery and so must have been painted in the first half of the year. The location is the beach at the foot of Beacon Hill cliffs with Clover Point in the distance.

Sketch relating to *Rushing Sea of Undergrowth*
99 oil on paper 88.6 x 59.7 cm, signed lower right: *M E CARR* [1935]
University College, University of Toronto
In June and September of 1935 Carr was in her van, camping at Albert Head, Metchosin, near Victoria. She describes this jungle experience in her Journals (HT, pp. 192-99).

A RUSHING SEA OF UNDERGROWTH
100 oil on canvas 111.8 x 68.6 cm, signed lower left: *EMILY CARR* [1935]
The Vancouver Art Gallery
The formalization of older trees in the blue background shows how Carr sometimes carried forward stylistic motifs from an earlier time; the related sketch is free of these. In October and November of 1935 she speaks in her Journals of the problem of capturing the jungle.

SCORNED AS TIMBER, BELOVED OF THE SKY
101 oil on canvas 111.8 x 68.4 cm, signed lower right: *M. E. CARR* [1935]
The Vancouver Art Gallery
Exhibited in February 1936 at the Library of the University of British Columbia, Vancouver, which almost certainly confirms a 1935 date.

A YOUNG TREE
102 oil on canvas 106.7 x 68.6 cm, signed lower right: *M.E. CARR* [1931]
The Vancouver Art Gallery

DEEP FOREST
103 oil on canvas 68.6 x 111.8 cm, signed lower right (white): *EMILY CARR*; lower left: *M E CARR* [c.1931-32]
The Vancouver Art Gallery

STUDY IN MOVEMENT
104 oil on canvas 68.6 x 111.8 cm, signed lower left: *EMILY CARR* [c.1935-36]
The Art Gallery of Ontario
This painting was included in an uncatalogued solo exhibition at the Art Gallery of Toronto, March-April 1937. On 30 April of that year Carr wrote in her Journal that the Toronto Art Gallery had purchased "Movement in the Woods" — no doubt this same painting — along with two others.

FOREST SKETCH
◁ oil on paper 61 x 91.6 cm, signed lower left: *EMILY CARR* [c.1935]
The Vancouver Art Gallery
Relates to *Study in Movement*, p. 128.

ABOVE THE TREES

105 oil on paper 127.3 x 60.8 cm, signed lower left: *EMILY CARR* [c.1939]
The Vancouver Art Gallery

Exhibited in Carr's exhibition at the Vancouver Art Gallery, November 1939 (no. 26, $50). Carr preferred to show new material which had not been seen before, especially on home territory, but this by no means proves a 1939 date. A stronger argument for a date later than 1935-36 is the unusual and bold form concept in which the whirling umbrella caps of the treetops echo, in their intense energy, the larger deep-blue dazzling cap of the sky.

THE MOUNTAIN

106 oil on canvas 111.4 x 68 cm, signed lower right: *M. EMILY CARR* [1933]
The McMichael Canadian Collection, Kleinburg, Ontario

This is certainly the canvas Carr refers to in her Journals (HT, pp. 38-40, 46, 47 and 67). She started the painting in July 1933, following her sketching trip in May and June of that year into the interior of the province north of Vancouver. She finished it in October.

HOUSES BELOW THE MOUNTAIN

107 oil on paper 91.4 x 60.3 cm, signed lower left: *EMILY CARR* [1933]
Government of the Province of Alberta

See note for *The Mountain*.

VILLAGE IN THE HILLS

◁ oil on canvas 68.6 x 111.6 cm, signed lower right: *M. EMILY CARR* [1933]
The Vancouver Art Gallery

SOMBRENESS SUNLIT

108 oil on canvas 111.9 x 68.6 cm, signed lower right: *EMILY CARR* [c.1937-40]
The Province of British Columbia, Provincial Archives

The very broad direct handling with its emphasis on light and rushing movement suggest a late date. A painting of this title was exhibited with the British Columbia Society of Fine Arts in Vancouver, May-June 1941. A painting bearing the same title is in the collection of the Art Gallery of Greater Victoria.

Three tufted treetops and sky (untitled)

109 oil on paper 91.3 x 60.2 cm, signed lower right: *EMILY CARR* [c.1939]
The Vancouver Art Gallery

The brush style in this painting closely resembles that in *Young Pines and Old Maples*, which was exhibited in November 1939 at the Vancouver Art Gallery. Both were probably done in September of that year when she was camping on Craigflower Road, where there were "tall firs, little pines, scrub, arbutus bushes and maples." (HT, p. 305)

ODDS AND ENDS

110 oil on canvas 67.3 x 109.5 cm, signed lower left: *EMILY CARR* [c.1939]
The Greater Victoria Public Library

See text, p. 122. This painting was exhibited in Carr's solo exhibition at the Vancouver Art Gallery in November 1939.

ABOVE THE GRAVEL PIT

111 oil on canvas 76.8 x 102.2 cm, signed lower right: *EMILY CARR* [1937]
The Vancouver Art Gallery

In June and September of 1936 Carr was camping at the "gravel pits" in Metchosin. A reference in her Journals, September 1937 (HT, p. 293) describes this painting very closely.

OVERHEAD

112 oil on paper 61 x 91.6 cm, signed lower right: *EMILY CARR* [c.1935-36]
The Vancouver Art Gallery

LILLOOET INDIAN VILLAGE

113 oil on canvas 68.3 x 91.1 cm, signed lower right: *EMILY CARR* [1933]
The Glenbow Museum, Calgary

Based on Carr's trip in June of 1933 into the interior of the province.

ROCKS BY THE SEA

◁ 114 oil on paper 59.7 x 86.36 cm, signed lower right: *EMILY CARR* [c.1939]
private collection

This painting has a conceptual affinity with *Above the Trees*: both tackle a daring and difficult composition in which there is no foreground relating the picture's space to the spectator's; both have similar blazing, spangled skies. The suggested date is speculative, based on the advanced concept of space employed. The likely reference to this work (quoted p. 135) from a late letter to Ira Dilworth, may or may not have relevance to the date.

TREES IN THE SKY

115 oil on canvas 111.76 x 68.58 cm, signed lower left: *EMILY CARR* [c.1939]
private collection

Sketch relating to *Scorned as Timber, Beloved of the Sky*

116 oil on paper 87.6 x 59.7 cm, signed lower right: *M. E. CARR* [1935]
private collection

THE PINE TREE

117 oil on paper 88.9 x 59.7 cm, signed lower right: *M E CARR* [probably 1935]
Art Gallery of Hamilton, gift of Gordon A. Davies in memory of his wife, Doris L. Davies of Toronto, 1978

In June 1935, and again in September, Carr was camping in her caravan at Albert Head, Metchosin. This and the preceding and following two sketches probably originated during one of those sketching sessions. In June she spoke of the importance of sky as an integral part of a picture's conception. (HT, p. 187)

EDGE OF THE FOREST

118 oil on paper 83.8 x 55.9 cm, signed lower right: *M E CARR* [probably 1935]
The McMichael Canadian Collection, Kleinburg, Ontario

This sketch bears an obvious relation to the previous one, but it is both more conceptually developed and more finished. It was either worked on in the studio or possibly entirely painted in the studio from the other sketch.

DANCING SUNLIGHT

119 oil on canvas 83.5 x 60.9 cm, signed lower right: *EMILY CARR* [c.1937-40]
The McMichael Canadian Collection, Kleinburg, Ontario

This is one of Carr's most freely painted canvases; like *Sombreness Sunlit* it carries forward into her late phase of animation the light-in-the-woods theme which had surfaced as early as 1909.

FOREST LIGHT

120 oil on canvas 54.6 x 54.7 cm, signed lower right: *M E CARR* [c.1931-32]
private collection

A black and white brush drawing in the collection of the Vancouver Art Gallery closely relates to this painting.

FOREST INTERIOR IN SHAFTS OF LIGHT

121 oil on canvas 86.7 x 76.5 cm, signed lower right: *EMILY CARR* [c.1935-37]
Fannin Hall Collection Ltd., Vancouver

The title is a recent identification for this painting, and dating is a matter of speculation. The mixture of approaches — the hair-like foliage in the foreground, the stylized tree and clump of trees middle ground left, the shafts of light, and the amount of over-painting — suggest that this is an earlier canvas worked over in an experimental mood. It is worth noting that in 1935 Carr observed that Lawren Harris had moved into abstraction. The zigzag shaft of light left of centre is flat and quite unlike the volumetric shafts of light in her 1930-31 skies like those in *Vanquished*.

FOREST

122 oil on canvas 129.1 x 76 cm, signed lower left: *EMILY CARR* [c.1931-33]
The Vancouver Art Gallery

The handling of foliage is of the same stylistic vintage as that in *Red Cedar*.

TREES, GOLDSTREAM FLATS

123 oil on canvas 91.1 x 68.58 cm, signed lower left: *EMILY CARR* [1931]
private collection
This, and a canvas in the Glenbow Museum collection on the same theme (light in the depths of the old forest) probably originated in the work done during Carr's sketching session in Goldstream Park near Victoria, September 1931.

BLUE SKY

124 oil on paper 95.3 x 66.14 cm, signed lower right: *EMILY CARR* [c.1932-34]
private collection
Carr described this painting to the owner at the time of purchase as "strong meat." The date is suggested on the basis of a concept of form that is relatively firm and dense.

WEST COAST FOREST OF GREAT TREES

125 oil on paper 88.90 x 58.42 cm, signed lower right: *M E CARR* [c. 1935-37/38]
private collection
Very similar to the painting which appears in the 1938 snapshot of Carr's studio (see note, no. 127).

CORDOVA DRIFT

126 oil on canvas 90.2 x 74.9 cm, signed lower right: *M EMILY CARR* [1931]
private collection
Probably painted in the summer or fall of 1931 following Carr's sketching session in May of that year.

CORDOVA BAY

◁ oil on paper 60 x 90.2 cm, signed lower left: *M E CARR* [1931]
The Vancouver Art Gallery
In May 1931 Carr was camping at Cordova Bay near Victoria. The oil-on-paper sketches of this season have very much the character of dry brush drawings in tone with colour added.

SHORE AND FOREST (Cordova Bay)

◁ oil on paper 60.96 x 68 cm, signed lower right: *M E CARR* [1931]
private collection
Painted during the same sketching session as the previous work.

WOOD INTERIOR

127 oil on canvas 129.9 x 86.2 cm, signed lower right: *EMILY CARR* [1932-1935]
The Vancouver Art Gallery

This major canvas presents unusual problems in dating. It shares its theme — lighted opening into deep woods, as well as the implied solidity of forms — with canvases of 1931-32. The handling of forest floor growth is close to that of *The Red Cedar*. But compared to *Forest, British Columbia*, for instance, the difference in Carr's perception of the woods is striking: the former sees woods in solid and somewhat theatrical terms, with light on the hanging draperies of foliage, trunks, etc. coming from an external source. In *Wood Interior* the emphasis has shifted from smoothly modelled forms and directed light to ambient light that flickers and glints over, through and around surfaces of trunks, and irradiates the forest core. Bold and differentiated brush strokes at times cut right across tree trunk outlines, and give the canvas a surface immediacy, despite volume and depth. A speculative solution to the problem would be to see this as an earlier canvas (1931-32) repainted in the light of a later perception, mid-way in a conceptual evolution between *Forest, British Columbia* and the freely painted *Sombreness Sunlit*, no. 108, which deals with the same theme.

Two works with the same title, *Wood Interior*, which appear in exhibition records, are not this painting: the one shown in March 1932 at the Roerich Museum in New York and at Atlantic City, summer 1933, was one of the formalized 1929-30 forest paintings, no. 75; and another by that name, shown with the Canadian Group of Painters in Toronto in January 1936 and in Ottawa in February, was an oil-on-paper sketch. The first time this canvas can be surely identified in an exhibition list is in Carr's solo exhibition at the Vancouver Art Gallery, October 1938, under the title *Solemn Big Woods*. A 1938 snapshot of Carr's studio (Cheney papers, Special Collections, U.B.C. Library) shows a sketch or painting very similar to one reproduced in the 1936 edition of *The Yearbook of the Arts in Canada* (edited by Bertram Brooker) and to this canvas.

RED CEDAR

128 oil on canvas 111 x 68.6 cm, signed lower right: *EMILY CARR* [c.1931-33]
The Vancouver Art Gallery

Although a *Red Cedar* was exhibited in December 1931 with the Group of Seven exhibition at the Art Gallery of Toronto, the luminous and painterly feeling for undergrowth and foliage in this canvas is hard to reconcile with that early date. Carr sketched among the cedars at Goldstream Flats in September 1931 and also in August-September of 1933, and the later date seems the more likely one to have produced the source material for this painting. It is also possible that the painting was done in 1931 and and partially repainted later.

BOLE OF A TREE

129 oil on paper 56.2 x 41 cm, signed lower left: *EMILY CARR* [c.1934-36]
private collection

There is a pasted inscription on the backing: "Autumn #4, $40."

Young tree in surging growth (untitled)

130 oil on paper 85.4 x 55.3 cm, signed lower left: *M EMILY CARR* [c.1936]
private collection

TREE

131 oil on paper 88.1 x 59.1 cm, signed lower left: *EMILY CARR* [1932 or 1933]
The Vancouver Art Gallery

REFORESTATION

132 oil on canvas 110 x 67.2 cm, signed and dated lower left: *M EMILY CARR 1936*
The McMichael Canadian Collection, Kleinburg, Ontario

YOUNG AND OLD FOREST, B.C. (Sketch relating to *Something Unnamed*)

133 oil on paper 91.4 x 60.3 cm, signed lower right centre: *EMILY CARR* [1936]
Dr. and Mrs. Max Stern, Dominion Gallery, Montreal

Carr was working on or from this sketch in January 1938 (see HT, p. 272). Since she was unable to do outdoor sketching in 1937, it was probably done in 1936.

REBIRTH (original title *Something Unnamed*)

134 oil on canvas 112.2 x 68.9 cm, signed lower left: *EMILY CARR* [1937]
Fannin Hall Collection Ltd., Vancouver

This canvas has been renamed *Rebirth*, but it was exhibited as *Something Unnamed* in Carr's solo exhibition at the Vancouver Art Gallery, November 1938 (no. 20, $225). A 1 January 1937 entry in her Journals (HT, p. 272) shows that she was working on it, or possibly the sketch for it, at that time. Probably the painting was finished later that year after she had recovered from her heart attack in January.

YOUNG ARBUTUS

135 oil on paper 83.8 x 53.3 cm, signed lower right: *EMILY CARR/VICTORIA* [suggested date September 1939]
private collection

Compare with *Laughing Forest* which shows affinities in mood and handling.

MIDSUMMER EVE

◁ oil on paper 42.2 x 56.8 cm, signed lower right: *EMILY CARR* [1938]
The Glenbow Museum, Calgary

In August 1938 Carr was sketching in a little shack at Telegraph Bay where she did over thirty sketches. (Ruth Humphrey in a letter to Nan Cheney, Special Collections, University of British Columbia Library) This sketch was exhibited in November 1938 at Carr's solo exhibition, Vancouver Art Gallery (no. 1, $35).

FOREST LANDSCAPE II

136 oil on paper 91.4 x 61 cm, signed lower right: *EMILY CARR* [c.1938-39]
The National Gallery of Canada

Windswept trees (untitled)

137   oil on paper 104.1 x 75 cm, signed lower left: *M.E. CARR* [probably 1936]
Maltwood Art Museum and Gallery, University of Victoria

See note for *Swirl*. Carr was unable to do outdoor sketching in 1937, and this sketch was probably done the year previously.

LAUGHING FOREST

138   oil on paper 59.7 x 90.2 cm, signed lower left: *EMILY CARR* [c.1939]
Fannin Hall Collection Ltd., Vancouver

In September 1939 Carr was sketching from a "little one-room shack on Craigflower Road." (HT, p. 305) This sketch may be from that session.

SWIRL

139   oil on canvas 68.3 x 57.8 cm, signed lower right: *EMILY CARR* [1937]
private collection

Swirl relates to both the small canvas *Juice of Life*, in the collection of the Art Gallery of Greater Victoria, and the untitled paper sketch of windswept trees. The latter is clearly a source for the two canvases, of which *Swirl* is the more developed. *Swirl* was exhibited with the Canadian Group of Painters exhibition in Toronto, November-December 1937, and is very likely the "exultant wood" she speaks of working on in April (HT, p. 288), and the "Sunshiny Woods" Mr. Band ordered sent to Toronto in September (HT, p. 293).

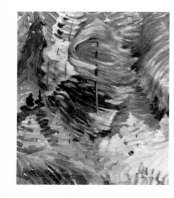

JUICE OF LIFE

◁   oil on canvas 64.5 x 54.7 cm, signed lower right: *EMILY CARR* [c.1936-37]
The Art Gallery of Greater Victoria

See note for *Swirl*.

YOUNG PINES AND SKY

140   oil on paper 89.2 x 58.3 cm, signed lower right: *EMILY CARR* [c.1935]
The Vancouver Art Gallery

B.C. TREES

141   oil on paper 88 x 58.5 cm, signed lower right: *M E CARR* [1934 or 1935]
Rolla and Peter Freygood

FOREST LANDSCAPE I

142   oil on paper 91.4 x 61 cm, signed lower right: *EMILY CARR* [suggested date June 1939]
The National Gallery of Canada

Carr was sketching at Langford in June 1939. An unpublished entry from her Journals (Public Archives of Canada) reads: "Langford Camp, June 8, Millstream Road . . . grey days in the mossy wood are very fine, a rich yellow gold carpet of moss and these straight, purplish tree stems with dull green tops. Very lovely." This, and the very free horizontal calligraphy, support a late date.

METCHOSIN

143   oil on paper 87.6 x 57.2 cm, signed lower right: *EMILY CARR* [1934 or 1935]
private collection

As far as dating is concerned, the title *Metchosin* by itself is not conclusive, as Carr sketched in different parts of that area on camping sessions in May and September of 1934, June and September of 1935, June and September 1936, and twice again in 1940. In June 1934, among her subjects were "stumps and pines and space" (HT, p. 132), and in September that same year, "high and blue sky, straggle of distant pines and stumps and dry grass in foreground, all soused in light and vibrating with glow" (HT, p. 148). In June 1935 at Albert Head she wrote: "There's a row of pine trees that won't leave me alone. They are straight across the field from the van. Second growth, pointed, fluffy and thick. . . . They are very green, and sky, high and blue, is behind them. On days like today the relationship between the trees and the sky is very close." (HT, p. 187) In this sketch and the several following, Carr's concern for the relationship between trees and sky is very apparent.

FOREST (tree trunks)

144   oil on paper 90.8 x 60.3 cm, estate stamp lower left [c.1939-40]
private collection

FOREST CLEARING (Langford)

145 oil on paper 60.3 x 91.4 cm, signed lower right: *EMILY CARR*   [1939]
The Art Gallery of Hamilton

The relation of this sketch to the canvas *Near Langford B.C.* indicates that it was done in June
of 1939 when she was sketching in that area.

NEAR LANGFORD B.C.

146 oil on canvas 68.5 x 101.6 cm, signed lower right: *EMILY CARR*   [1939]
private collection

Exhibited in Carr's solo exhibition, November 1939, at the Vancouver Art Gallery (no. 14, $250).

LOGGERS' CULLS

147 oil on canvas 69 x 112 cm, signed and dated lower right: *M. EMILY CARR 1935*
The Vancouver Art Gallery

STUMPS AND SKY

148 oil on paper 58.4 x 90.2 cm, signed lower right: *M. E. CARR* [probably 1934]
The Art Gallery of Ontario, gift from the Douglas M. Duncan collection, 1970

In May and June, and again in September, Carr was camping off Metchosin Road (see quotations
from her Journals of 1934 under *Metchosin*, no. 143, which fit this sketch well). A year later,
19 September 1935, while camping and sketching near Albert Head in Metchosin, she made a remark
that evokes this sketch and many others in which she uses whirling circular forms in the sky: "It is
done in swirly rings. Why? Not for affectation any more than the cubists squared for affectation.
Like them I was trying to get planes but used disks instead of cubes." (HT, p. 196)

PLUMED FIRS

◁ 149 oil on canvas 65.4 x 99.1 cm, signed lower right: *EMILY CARR*   [c.1939-41]
University of British Columbia

The direct, relatively unfinished and bold calligraphic handling of paint in this canvas suggest a late
date. A canvas close in style to this, *Bounce of Spring*, was exhibited in October-November 1941
at the Vancouver Art Gallery.

MOUNTAIN FOREST

150 oil on canvas 112.1 x 68.7 cm, signed lower right: *EMILY CARR*   [1935 or 1936]
The Vancouver Art Gallery

CHILL DAY IN JUNE

151 oil on paper 106 x 75 cm, signed lower right: *EMILY CARR*   [c.1938-39]
The Maltwood Art Museum and Gallery, University of Victoria

The rippling foliage and horizontally stroked tree trunks, as well as the moisture-laden atmosphere
and colour, suggest a date corresponding to that of the National Gallery's *Forest Landscape I*.

Light woods in spring (untitled)

152 oil on paper 86.7 x 55.9 cm, signed and dated lower left: *EMILY CARR 1940*
private collection

In May 1940 Carr was sketching near Colwood in the Metchosin area near Victoria. Of the work she
did on that trip she said: "I have got the sketches out that I did on the trip just before my stroke
[5 June]. They are very full of spring joy, high in key, with lots of light and tenderness of spring.
How did I do these joyous things when I was so torn up over the war? . . . when I went into the woods
I could rise and skip with the spring and forget my bad heart." (HT, pp. 324-25) This painting has
been varnished, which accounts for the orange tonality. It is one of the very few dated oil-on-paper
paintings.

STUMPS AND SKY

153 oil on paper 59.1 x 90.2 cm, signed lower right: *EMILY CARR*   [probably 1934]
The Vancouver Art Gallery

LANGFORD, B.C. (sketch relating to *Plumed Firs*)

◁ 154 oil on paper 57.2 x 87.6 cm, signed lower right: *EMILY CARR*   [c.1939]
The Edmonton Art Gallery

The title by which this sketch was previously known, *Mountain Landscape*, was changed to *Langford* when the author pointed out its similarity to *Forest Clearing* and to the related canvas *Near Langford, B.C.*

FIR TREE AND SKY
155   oil on canvas 111.76 x 68 cm, signed lower right: *M E CARR* [1935-36]
private collection
The description Carr gives in HT, p. 170, almost certainly is of this painting. The entry comes under the date 9 February 1935, but it may be part of a misplaced section in the Journals. The painting was probably done in the fall of 1935 or early 1936.

SWAYING
156   oil on canvas 34.6 x 45.7 cm, signed lower left: *EMILY CARR* [c.1935-36]
The McMichael Canadian Collection, Kleinburg, Ontario

FOREST LANDSCAPE
157   oil on paper 87.8 x 58.5 cm, signed lower right: *EMILY CARR* [c.1935-36]
private collection
The differentiation and independent vitality of the brush strokes suggest a date around the middle of the decade. The sketch is unusually well covered and finished — probably worked on in her studio. "Beckley St.," the address to which she moved in early March 1936, is written on the back.

FOREST
158   oil on canvas 111.8 x 68.58 cm, signed lower right: *EMILY CARR* [c.1937]
Board of Regents, Victoria University, University of Toronto
On 4 August 1937 Carr wrote in her Journal, "I worked on . . . the inside of a woods, up a hill. . . . it all depends on the sweep and swirl and I have not got it yet." (HT, p. 293) This quotation appears to fit this painting and could be a clue to its date. The style and colour resemble that of *Swaying*.

Light in the "jungle" (untitled)
◁ 159   oil on canvas 84.8 x 74.6 cm, signed lower left: *EMILY CARR* [c.1937-40]
private collection
This is one of Carr's most freely painted canvases. In certain late works like this, the canvas retains much of the spontaneity and freshness found in the sketch.

YELLOW MOSS
160   oil on canvas 68.58 x 102.9 cm, signed lower left: *EMILY CARR* [1939]
private collection
Probably based on work done on Carr's sketching trip to Langford, June 1939. In an unpublished passage from her Journals (Public Archives of Canada) she speaks of "a rich yellow gold carpet of moss." It was exhibited in her solo exhibition at the Vancouver Art Gallery in November 1939 (no. 21, $200).

ROOTS
161   oil on canvas 112 x 69 cm, signed lower right: *EMILY CARR* [c.1937-39]
The Province of British Columbia, Provincial Archives
The free flame-like handling of trees and sky are similar to that in *Yellow Moss*, a canvas which was exhibited in November 1939 at the Vancouver Art Gallery.

SKY
162   oil on paper 57.1 x 88.9 cm, signed lower right: *M E CARR* [c.1935-36]
The National Gallery of Canada

SEASCAPE
163   oil on paper 57 x 85.2 cm, signed lower left: *M E CARR* [c.1936]
private collection

STRAIT OF JUAN DE FUCA
164   oil on paper 59.1 x 86.36 cm, signed (twice) lower right: *EMILY CARR / M E CARR* [c.1934]
private collection

Whiffen Spit near Sooke (untitled)
165　oil on paper 57.2 x 86.36 cm, signed lower right: M E CARR　[c.1935-36]
private collection

STRAIT OF JUAN DE FUCA
166　oil on paper 56.2 x 87 cm, signed lower right: M E CARR　[c.1936]
The Edmonton Art Gallery, gift of Mrs. Max Stern, Dominion Gallery, Montreal

Clover Point from Dallas Road beach (untitled)
167　oil on paper 55.88 x 87.6 cm, signed lower right: EMILY CARR　[c.1934-36]
private collection

FORSAKEN
168　oil on canvas 117.5 x 75.6 cm, signed lower right: EMILY CARR　[1937]
The Vancouver Art Gallery

On 14 April 1937 Carr wrote in her Journal, "I have been painting a Nass pole in a sea of green" (HT, p. 286), and on 20 April, "I have been painting all day . . . Nass pole in undergrowth" (HT, p. 288). The pole represented here is from the Tsimshian village of Angidah on the Nass River and today is in the National Museum of Man, Ottawa. See also Barbeau, *Totem Poles*, vol. 1, p. 231. There are source sketches of this pole by Carr in the Newcombe Collection in Victoria. The overlapping conical trees in the middle left are a stylistic throwback from earlier work. Carr had barely recovered from a severe heart attack in January 1937 when she painted this in April.

A SKIDEGATE POLE
169　oil on canvas 86.4 x 76.2 cm, signed lower right: EMILY CARR　[1941-42]
The Vancouver Art Gallery

SKIDEGATE (shark pole)
◁　oil on card 64.2 x 31.8 cm, signed, inscribed and dated lower right: M. *EMILY CARR/ SKIDIGATE 1912*
The Vancouver Art Gallery

The subject is a Haida pole of the shark at Skidegate. See Barbeau, *Totem Poles*, vol. 1, p. 102, fig. 31.

LAUGHING BEAR
170　oil on paper 76.6 x 55.3 cm, signed lower left: EMILY CARR　[1941]
private collection

Carr painted this for her publishers, Mr. and Mrs. W. Clarke, in 1941 in connection with the publication of *Klee Wyck*. On p. 53 of *Klee Wyck*, Carr mistakenly identifies the location as Gittex; it is Angidah. The pole can be seen from the front view in a photograph in Barbeau's *Totem Poles*, vol. 1, p. 230.

MASSET BEARS
171　oil on canvas 101.3 x 44.5 cm, signed lower left: EMILY CARR　[c.1941]
The Vancouver Art Gallery

Carr spoke of working on the "Massett bear" in her Journal, 20 April 1937 (HT, p. 288), probably a painting in the Province of British Columbia's collection in Victoria. This painting was most likely done in 1941, along with other Indian works. See text p. 180.

A SKIDEGATE BEAVER POLE
172　oil on canvas 86.2 x 76 cm, signed lower right: EMILY CARR　[1941-42]
The Vancouver Art Gallery

SKIDEGATE (beaver pole)
◁　oil on card 64.5 x 32.5 cm, signed, inscribed and dated lower left: M *EMILY CARR/ SKIDIGATE 1912*
The Vancouver Art Gallery

The subject is a Haida beaver pole of Skidegate. See the photograph in Barbeau's *Totem Poles*, vol. 1, p. 121.

CLEARING
173　oil on canvas 68.6 x 111.8 cm, signed and dated lower right: EMILY CARR 1942
The National Gallery of Canada

See Carr's autobiography, *Growing Pains*, pp. 279-80, for her recollection of the springtime when this canvas was painted.

CEDAR

174   oil on canvas 111.8 x 68.6 cm, signed and dated lower left: *EMILY CARR 1942*
The Vancouver Art Gallery

QUIET

175   oil on canvas 111.76 x 68.58 cm, signed and dated lower right: *EMILY CARR/ 1942*
private collection

CEDAR SANCTUARY

176   oil on paper 91.2 x 61 cm, signed lower right: *EMILY CARR* [c.1942]
The Vancouver Art Gallery

In a 1942 letter to Ira Dilworth (Public Archives of Canada) Carr writes: "Emily has *not* got the cedar rhythm yet nor their particular idiom. This place is full of cedars. Their colors are terribly sensitive to change of time and light — sometimes they are *bluish* cold green, then they turn yellow warm-green — sometimes their bows [sic] flop heavy and sometimes float, then they are fairy as ferns and then down they droop, heavy as heartaches." This sketch does not resemble those done in Mount Douglas Park which are more loosely painted, less finished and dated 1942. This may be at least partly a studio painting.

SELF-PORTRAIT

177   oil on paper 86.36 x 58.42 cm, signed lower right: *EMILY CARR* [1938-39]
private collection

Carr was painting portraits in the winter of 1938-39. See text p.

MY COOK (portrait of Shirley Bennett)

◁   oil on paper 86.36 x 57.2 cm, signed lower right: *EMILY CARR* [1938-39]
private collection

The sitter for this painting wrote to the owner that it is one of three studies of her done while she was working for Carr during the winter of 1938-39.

Photos

I   Emily Carr in her studio. In the background *Sunshine and Tumult*.
Photo by Harold Mortimer Lamb. Courtesy The Vancouver Art Gallery.

II   Carr as a young girl between 1889 and 1895

III   Carr in the Cariboo region of British Columbia, probably in the fall of 1904 on her way home from England.

IV   Family Picnic, 1889 — Emily, hands folded, seated on log, upper right; Richard, holding straw hat, reclining right foreground; "Lizzie" behind Richard holding child; Alice kneeling in front of log on left.

V   End papers: Carr sketching at Tanoo in 1912.
Courtesy of Ethnology Division, Provincial Museum of British Columbia.

REFERENCE NOTES

PROLOGUE

1 Emily Carr, *Hundreds and Thousands: The Journals of Emily Carr* (Toronto: Clarke, Irwin & Co., 1966), p. 206.

2 Carr to Dilworth, c. 1941-42, Emily Carr Papers (MG 30, D 215), Public Archives of Canada, Ottawa.
(All subsequent references to the Public Archives of Canada are from these papers.)

3 Emily Carr, *Growing Pains: The Autobiography of Emily Carr* (Toronto: Clarke, Irwin & Co., 1966), p. 5.

4 *Growing Pains*, p. 203.

5 *Hundreds and Thousands*, pp. 141-42.

6 *Hundreds and Thousands*, p. 238.

7 *Hundreds and Thousands*, p. 108.

8 *Hundreds and Thousands*, p. 145.

9 *Hundreds and Thousands*, p. 24.

10 *Hundreds and Thousands*, p. 289.

11 *Hundreds and Thousands*, p. 224.

THE BACKGROUND

1 Carr to Brown, 26 March 1939, National Gallery of Canada files, Ottawa.

2 Richard Carr's diary is in the Provincial Archives of British Columbia, Victoria.

3 Carr, *Growing Pains*, p. 14.

4 *Growing Pains*, p. 15.

5 *Growing Pains*, p. 12.

6 *Growing Pains*, p. 11.

7 Journals of Emily Carr [unpublished entry], Easter Monday, 1935, Public Archives of Canada, Ottawa.

8 Ibid.

9 Carr to Dilworth, probably 1942, Public Archives of Canada, Ottawa.

EARLY ACCOMPLISHMENTS

1 Carr, *Growing Pains*, p. 18.

2 *Growing Pains*, p. 49.

3 *Growing Pains*, p. 26.

4 *Growing Pains*, p. 73.

5 A note in the Public Archives of Canada by Ira Dilworth, quoting from Alice Carr's diary, states that Emily's first visit to Ucluelet took place when she was fifteen; this confirms Carr's own account in *Klee Wyck*.

6 *Growing Pains*, pp. 76, 80.

7 *Growing Pains*, p. 81.

8 *Growing Pains*, p. 154.

9 *Growing Pains*, p. 157.

10 *Growing Pains*, p. 176.

11 *Growing Pains*, p. 181.

12 *Growing Pains*, p. 200.

13 *Growing Pains*, p. 76.

14 Emily Carr, *Klee Wyck* (Toronto: Clarke, Irwin & Co., 1971), p. 4.

15 *Growing Pains*, p. 211.

16 *Growing Pains*, pp. 211-12.

FRENCH INFLUENCE

1 Carr, *Growing Pains*, p. 215.

2 Ibid.

3 *Growing Pains*, p. 216.

4 The studio of a Scotsman, John Ferguson, who also exhibited in the Paris *Salon d'Automne* of 1911.

5 Carr refers to an "Australian" watercolourist in *Growing Pains*, p. 226.

6 "Fresh Seeing" was the title of a talk Carr gave in Victoria, March 1930, to the Victoria Women's Canadian Club. Also the title of a book of two lectures by Carr (Toronto: Clarke, Irwin & Co., 1972).

7 See Dennis Reid, *A Concise History of Canadian Painting* (Toronto: Oxford University Press, 1973), p. 155: "It represented the most advanced and most accomplished experimental painting to be seen in Canada in 1912."

8 The lecture is in two notebooks in the Public Archives of Canada; the first is headed "Lecture on Totems" and on p. 53 of the second is the date April 1913.

9 *The Vancouver Daily Province*, 8 April 1912.

10 *Growing Pains*, p. 230.

11 Carr to Dilworth, c. 1942, Public Archives of Canada, Ottawa.

12 *Growing Pains*, p. 231.

13 Ibid.

14 *Growing Pains*, p. 232.

CARR AT THE TURNING POINT

1 Lamb to Brown, National Gallery of Canada files, Ottawa.

2 Carr, *Growing Pains*, p. 234.

3 Eric Brown in the introduction to the catalogue of the exhibition.

4 Carr, *Hundreds and Thousands*, p. 17.

5 *Hundreds and Thousands*, p. 8.

6 *Growing Pains*, p. 237.

THE MATURE YEARS COMMENCE

1 Carr, *Growing Pains*, p. 75.

2 Carr, *Hundreds and Thousands*, p. 8.

3 *Hundreds and Thousands*, p. 7.

4 Ibid.

5 Carr speaks of a "three-year struggle," apparently dating her start with theosophy in 1931; actually it commenced when she first met Harris in 1927, and ended in January 1934 when she wrote him "snapping the theosophy bond."

6 *Hundreds and Thousands*, p. 29.

7 Harris to Carr, Public Archives of Canada, Ottawa.

8 Carr to Dilworth, 14 February c. 1941, Public Archives of Canada, Ottawa.

9 *Hundreds and Thousands*, pp. 148-49.

10 *Hundreds and Thousands*, p. 208.

11 *Hundreds and Thousands*, p. 80.

12 *Hundreds and Thousands*, p. 94.

13 *Hundreds and Thousands*, p. 93.

14 *Hundreds and Thousands*, p. 95.

15 *Hundreds and Thousands*, p. 329.

16 *Hundreds and Thousands*, p. 15.

17 Ibid.

18 Harris to Carr, Public Archives of Canada, Ottawa.

19 *Growing Pains*, p. 240.

20 Carr to Brown, 1 October 1928, National Gallery of Canada files, Ottawa.

21 *Hundreds and Thousands*, p. 21. The original entry in the Public Archives of Canada, dated 24 November 1930, includes the somewhat

cryptic addition following "reversals of detail," "plain/action —
quiet/quick — action," suggesting that Carr had some difficulty in
understanding Tobey's instructions.

22 From author's conversation with Viola Patterson. She and her husband,
Ambrose, were two of Carr's artist acquaintances from Seattle.

23 Colin Graham to Donald Buchanan, 19 July 1957, National Gallery of
Canada files, Ottawa.

24 Mark Tobey in an interview with Audrey St. D. Johnston, *The Victoria
Daily Times*, 25 March 1957.

25 Carr to Brown, 11 August 1928, from South Bay, Skidegate, National
Gallery of Canada files, Ottawa.

A FORMAL PERIOD

1 See William C. Seitz, *Mark Tobey* (New York: The Museum of Modern
Art, 1962), pp. 45-47.

2 Emily Carr, "Lecture on Totems," April 1913, Public Archives of
Canada, Ottawa.

3 See Maria Tippett, *Emily Carr's "Blunden Harbour,"* National Gallery
of Canada Bulletin no. 25 (Ottawa: National Gallery of Canada, 1975)
and Edythe Hembroff-Schleicher, *m.e. A Portrayal of Emily Carr*
(Toronto: Clarke, Irwin & Co., 1969), pp. 55-56.

4 Carr, *Hundreds and Thousands*, p. 28.

5 It was Marius Barbeau who said that Tobey told Carr "to leave out
Indians and poles and paint from inside herself," advice that resulted in
Carr's quarrelling with Tobey and her feeling that he had rejected her.
(From the transcript of a CBC recording dated 1957, a copy of which is in
the National Gallery of Canada files, Ottawa.)

WIDER CONTACTS/TECHNICAL CHANGES

1 Carr to Brown, 19 October 1934, National Gallery of Canada files,
Ottawa.

2 Carr, *Hundreds and Thousands*, pp. 176-77.

3 Carr to Cheney, 11 October 1938, Nan Cheney Papers, Special
Collections, University of British Columbia Library, Vancouver.

4 Carr to Dilworth, Public Archives of Canada, Ottawa.

5 *Hundreds and Thousands*, p. 193.

6 Carr to Brown, 2 March 1937, National Gallery of Canada files, Ottawa.

7 For an account of this technique see Edythe Hembroff-Schleicher
(Carr's sketching companion), *m.e. A Portrayal*, pp. 41-42.

8 Carr to Brown, 4 March 1937, National Gallery of Canada files, Ottawa.

9 *Hundreds and Thousands*, p. 107.

10 *Hundreds and Thousands*, p. 204. The emphasized passage appears in
Carr's original Journal but not in the edited version.

11 *Hundreds and Thousands*, p. 216: a remark Carr made when she had
decided to leave the House of All Sorts and was in the process of
house-hunting.

12 *Hundreds and Thousands*, pp. 133-34.

A NEW LIBERATION

1 Carr, *Hundreds and Thousands*, p. 16.

2 *Hundreds and Thousands*, p. 185.

3 *Hundreds and Thousands*, p. 35.

4 References to Carr's struggle with *The Mountain* appear on pp. 45, 46, 47,
61, and 67 of *Hundreds and Thousands*.

5 *Hundreds and Thousands*, p. 45.

6 *Hundreds and Thousands*, p. 46.

A NEW INTEGRATION

1 Carr to Dilworth, 1941 or 1942, Public Archives of Canada, Ottawa.

2 Carr, *Hundreds and Thousands*, p. 133.

3 *Hundreds and Thousands*, p. 46.

4 *Hundreds and Thousands*, p. 47.

5 *Hundreds and Thousands*, p. 130.

6 *Hundreds and Thousands*, pp. 241-42.

7 *Hundreds and Thousands*, p. 101.

8 Carr, *Growing Pains*, pp. 259-60.

9 *Hundreds and Thousands*, p. 294.

LAST PERIOD

1 Carr, *Hundreds and Thousands*, p. 21.

2 *Hundreds and Thousands*, p. 288.

3 Carr to Cheney, Nan Cheney Papers, Special Collections, University of
British Columbia Library, Vancouver.

4 The exhibition was to be called "The Growth of an Artist" and was
discussed with W.H. Clarke, officials of the National Gallery, and a few
of Carr's fellow-artists — Harris, Holgate, Macdonald, Pepper, and
Jackson.

5 Carr to Ruth Humphrey, 6 July 1941, "Letters from Emily Carr,"
University of Toronto Quarterly 41 (Winter 1972):93-150.

6 Carr to Cheney, 7 February 1932, Nan Cheney Papers.

7 Carr to Cheney, 20 March 1932, Nan Cheney Papers.

8 *Hundreds and Thousands*, p. 301.

9 Humphrey to Cheney, 7 June 1940, Nan Cheney Papers.

10 *Hundreds and Thousands*, p. 330.

11 Carr to Walter Gage, 14 May 1943, Public Archives of Canada, Ottawa.

EPILOGUE

1 The People's Art Gallery was discussed in correspondence with Eric
Brown, National Gallery of Canada files, Ottawa.

2 Carr, *Hundreds and Thousands*, pp. 147-48.

3 *Hundreds and Thousands*, p. 287.

4 *Hundreds and Thousands*, pp. 76-77.

5 Carr to Brown, 4 March 1937, National Gallery of Canada files, Ottawa.

6 An exception is the work of William Blake, which Carr went to see
twice at the Art Institute on her trip to Chicago in 1933. See *Hundreds
and Thousands*, p. 75: "Blake knew how!"

7 *Hundreds and Thousands*, p. 106.

8. *Hundreds and Thousands*, p. 315.

9 *Hundreds and Thousands*, p. 30.

10 *Hundreds and Thousands*, p. 209.

SELECTED BIBLIOGRAPHY

Barbeau, Marius. *Totem Poles*. National Museum Bulletin 119. Ottawa: National Museum, 1950-51.

Buchanan, Donald W. "Emily Carr (1871-1945): An Expressionist among the Totem Poles." In *The Growth of Canadian Painting*, with a foreword by Eric Newton, pp. 48-50. London: Collins, 1950.

Buchanan, Donald W. "Emily Carr: Canadian Painter." *Studio* 126 (August 1943):60.

Buchanan, Donald W. "The Gentle and the Austere — A Comparison in Landscape Painting." *University of Toronto Quarterly* 11 (October 1941):72-77.

Burns, Flora Hamilton. "Emily Carr." In *The Clear Spirit: Twenty Canadian Women and Their Times*, edited by Mary Quayle Innis, pp. 221-41. Toronto: University of Toronto Press, 1966.

Burns, Flora Hamilton. "Emily Carr and the Newcombe Collection." *The Beaver*, Outfit 293 (Summer 1962):27-35.
> Reprinted as a catalogue, *The World of Emily Carr*, for the Hudson's Bay Company's exhibition at the Victoria and Vancouver stores, July-August 1962.

Canadian Painting in the Thirties. Compiled by Charles C. Hill. Ottawa: National Gallery of Canada, 1975.

Carr, Emily. *An Address*. With an introduction by Ira Dilworth. Toronto: Oxford University Press, 1955.

Carr, Emily. *A Little Town and a Little Girl*. With a foreword by Ira Dilworth. Toronto: Clarke, Irwin & Co., 1951.

Carr, Emily. *Fresh Seeing: Two Addresses by Emily Carr*. With a preface by Doris Shadbolt and an introduction to the 1930 speech by Ira Dilworth. Toronto: Clarke, Irwin & Co., 1972.

Carr, Emily. *Growing Pains: The Autobiography of Emily Carr*. With a foreword by Ira Dilworth. 2nd ed. Toronto: Clarke, Irwin & Co., 1966.

Carr, Emily. *Hundreds and Thousands: The Journals of Emily Carr*. 2nd ed. Toronto: Clarke, Irwin & Co., 1966.
> A numbered, limited edition of 1000 copies in large format, slipcased, with a folio of twelve hand-mounted prints, facsimile page and essays by Lawren Harris and Ira Dilworth was published as well as the regular edition.

Carr, Emily. *Klee Wyck*. With a foreword by Ira Dilworth. 5th ed. Toronto: Clarke, Irwin & Co., 1971.

Carr, Emily. "Letters from Emily Carr [to Ruth Humphrey, 1937 to 1944]." *University of Toronto Quarterly* 41 (Winter 1972):93-150.

Carr, Emily. "Modern and Indian Art of the West Coast." Supplement to *The McGill News*, June 1929, pp. 18-22.

Carr, Emily. *Pause: A Sketch Book*. 2nd ed. Toronto: Clarke, Irwin & Co., 1972.

Carr, Emily. *The Book of Small*. 2nd ed. Toronto: Clarke, Irwin & Co., 1966.

Carr, Emily. *The Heart of a Peacock*. Edited by Ira Dilworth. Toronto: Oxford University Press, 1953.

Carr, Emily. *The House of All Sorts*. 3rd ed. Toronto: Clarke, Irwin & Co., 1971.

Colman, M.E. "Emily Carr and Her Sisters." *Dalhousie Review* 27 (April 1947):29-32.

Contemporaries of Emily Carr in British Columbia. Catalogue for the Simon Fraser Gallery exhibition, 1974. Introduction by Maria Tippett. Burnaby: Simon Fraser University, 1974.

Daniells, Roy. "Emily Carr." In *Our Living Tradition*, 4th Series, edited by Robert L. McDougall, pp. 119-34. Toronto: University of Toronto Press, 1962.

Dilworth, Ira. "Emily Carr — Canadian Artist-Author." *Saturday Night*, 1 November 1941, p. 26.

Dilworth, Ira. "Emily Carr — Canadian Painter and Poet in Prose." *Saturday Night*, 8 November 1941, p. 26.

Emily Carr, a Centennial Exhibition Celebrating the One Hundredth Anniversary of Her Birth. Catalogue prepared by Doris Shadbolt. Rev. ed. Vancouver: J.J. Douglas, 1975.

Emily Carr: Her Paintings and Sketches. With articles by Ira Dilworth and Lawren Harris. Ottawa: National Gallery of Canada, 1945.

Exhibition of Canadian West Coast Art: Native and Modern. Ottawa: National Gallery of Canada, 1927.

Fenton, Terry. "Two Isolated Modernists [David Milne and Emily Carr]." In *Modern Painting in Canada: Major Movements in Twentieth Century Canadian Art*, by Terry Fenton and Karen Wilkin, p. 47. Edmonton: Hurtig Publishers, 1978.
> Also appeared as a catalogue for an exhibition organized by the Edmonton Art Gallery and held there 7 July to 30 August 1978.

Harris, Lawren. "Emily Carr and Her Work." *The Canadian Forum* 21 (December 1941):277-78.

Hembroff-Schleicher, Edythe. *Emily Carr: The Untold Story*. Saanichton, B.C.: Hancock House, 1978.
> A limited, numbered, and signed donor's edition includes a numbered facsimile edition of "Billie's Calendar."

Hembroff-Schleicher, Edythe. *m.e. A Portrayal of Emily Carr*. Toronto: Clarke, Irwin & Co., 1969.

Lippard, Lucy. "Quite Contrary: Body, Nature, Ritual in Women's Art." *Chrysalis*, no. 2 (1977), pp. 31-47.

Lord, Barry. "The Achievement of Emily Carr." In *The History of Painting in Canada: Toward a People's Art*, pp. 173-78. Toronto: NC Press, 1974.

McInnes, Graham [Campbell]. "L'Art d'Emily Carr." *Gants du Ciel*, no. 9 (Automne 1945), pp. 61-72.

McInnes, G[raham] Campbell. "World of Art." *Saturday Night*, 7 December 1935, p. 27.

Ottawa. National Gallery of Canada. Emily Carr correspondence.

Ottawa. Public Archives of Canada, MG 30, D 215. Emily Carr papers: original journals; correspondence to and from Ira Dilworth; from Lawren Harris; miscellaneous notes and correspondence.

Reid, Dennis, "Emily Carr, LeMoine Fitzgerald, and David Milne, 1912-1950." In *A Concise History of Canadian Painting*, pp. 153-72. Toronto: Oxford University Press, 1973.

Stacton, David Derek. "The Art of Emily Carr." *Queen's Quarterly* 57 (Winter 1950-51):499-509.

The Mature Years. Catalogue for the 1979 exhibition, Canada House Gallery, London. Introduction by Doris Shadbolt. Vancouver: Vancouver Art Gallery, 1979.

Thom, William Wylie. "Emily Carr in Vancouver: 1906-1913." In "The Fine Arts in Vancouver, 1886-1930: An Historical Survey," pp. 59-76. Master's Thesis, University of British Columbia, 1969.

Tippett, Maria. "A Paste Solitaire in a Steel-Claw Setting: Emily Carr and Her Public." *B.C. Studies*, no. 20 (Winter 1973-74), pp. 3-14.

Tippett, Maria. *Emily Carr's "Blunden Harbour."* National Gallery of Canada Bulletin, no. 25 (1975), pp. 33-37.

Tippett, Maria. "Emily Carr's *Klee Wyck*." *Canadian Literature*, no. 72 (Spring 1977), pp. 49-58.

Tippett, Maria. "Who 'Discovered' Emily Carr?" *Journal of Canadian Art History* 1 (Fall 1974):30-34.

Tippett, Maria, and Cole, Douglas. "The First Conscious Expression of the Rhythm of Life: Emily Carr." In *From Desolation to Splendour: Changing Perceptions of the British Columbia Landscape,* pp. 91-102. Toronto: Clarke, Irwin & Co., 1977.

Turpin, Marguerite. *The Life and Work of Emily Carr (1871-1945): A Selected Bibliography.* Western Canadian Contributions to Librarianship, no. 2. Vancouver: School of Librarianship, University of British Columbia, 1965.

Vancouver. University of British Columbia. Library, Special Collections. Nan Cheney papers.

Victoria. Provincial Archives of British Columbia. Emily Carr correspondence (photocopies of material stored at the Public Archives of Canada, Ottawa).

Victoria. Provincial Archives of British Columbia. Richard Carr's diary.

27/3/80